GAMES FOR WRITING

Also by Peggy Kaye

GAMES FOR MATH

GAMES FOR READING

GAMES FOR LEARNING

GAMES FOR WRITING

PLAYFUL WAYS TO HELP
YOUR CHILD LEARN TO WRITE

WRITTEN BY **Peggy Kaye**

WITH ILLUSTRATIONS
BY THE AUTHOR

FARRAR, STRAUS & GIROUX

NEW YORK

Farrar, Straus and Giroux
18 West 18th Street, New York 10011

Copyright © 1995 by Peggy Kaye
All rights reserved
Distributed in Canada by Douglas & McIntyre Ltd.
Printed in the United States of America
Published simultaneously in hardcover by Farrar, Straus and Giroux
First edition, 1995

Library of Congress Cataloging-in-Publication Data
Kaye, Peggy, 1948–
    Games for writing : playful ways to help your child learn to write / written by
Peggy Kaye ; with illustrations by the author.— 1st ed.
        p.   cm.
    ISBN-13: 978-0-374-52427-2
    ISBN-10: 0-374-52427-0
    1. Children—Writing.   2. Educational games.   I. Title.

LB1139.W7 K39 1995
372.6'23—dc20

                                                            94040745

www.fsgbooks.com

23   22   21   20   19

ACKNOWLEDGMENTS

The games in this book were tested and evaluated by a select team of experts—my students. I thank them for their unfailing honesty. Thanks also to Sara Bershtel for her judgment and insight, Elisabeth Kallick Dyssegaard for jumping in so expertly, and Edward Cohen. I was very lucky to have the benefit of Elizabeth Kaye's writing talent.

As always, Paul Berman's help is everything.

This book is dedicated to my mother, Lynn Lane, who understood the proper place of proper spelling.

CONTENTS

PART THREE: BUGABOOS—SPELLING, HANDWRITING, AND GRAMMAR   83

PART FOUR: WRITING WITH STYLE   119

INTRODUCTION

Writing is so hard to do that human society existed for untold eons before anyone gave it a try. After many thousands of years, civilization arose in Ancient Sumer and Egypt and the principles of writing were finally invented. But even then, and for the next several millennia, only select individuals learned to inscribe a few words in clay, carve them in stone, or ink them on papyrus. Today we expect everyone to write, and not only that, we expect them to do it before they are nine years old.

Yet writing hasn't become any easier. There are dozens of challenging rules to master. There are spelling, penmanship, and punctuation rules. There are rules about composition, too. Writers must think about the best way to begin a piece of writing and the most effective way to end it. They must figure out how to make sense of and squeeze in all the necessary information while leaving out the unnecessary. These skills were difficult to master in the time of the Ptolemies, and they are just as troublesome today.

Is it any wonder, then, that the schoolroom is sometimes a place of struggle? The task confronting children is huge. They must work hard. They need help. With the right approach, adults can offer that help, and they can do so without uttering threats or putting children through repetitive drills. For, by a lucky quirk of human nature, children sometimes enjoy doing the very things that are best for them, and one of those things is to play educationally useful games. Children take pleasure both in competitive games played for points and in noncompetitive games played just for fun. Games put children in a mood of alertness and concentration, which is exactly the right mood for learning. The children become positively eager to learn—not minding the skill that needs to be mastered is very difficult.

In my work as a teacher and tutor, I constantly take advantage of well-designed educational games, and I encourage parents to do likewise. In *Games for Writing* you will find fifty-two games that will help your child develop the exact skills he or she needs to become a proficient writer.

How Children Become Writers

The process of learning to write begins years before a child enters first grade. The learning accelerates in elementary school, proceeds in junior and senior high, advances in college, and often continues throughout post-school adult life. Following the early writing career of one child is a good way to discover exactly what it takes to become a writer. Allow me, therefore, to introduce Debby, a typical child.

At age three, Debby is in her room at home surrounded by stuffed animals. She is telling a story, talking nonstop. Her animals are the characters, and Debby speaks for them. She can imagine hundreds of adventures, and so her story goes on and on. Telling stories isn't the same as writing, certainly, but the process of telling tales does lead a child to writing, when the time is right.

Debby turns four. Today she is drawing a picture. She has drawn many pictures in her life, but this one is different. This time Debby is telling a story aloud while she draws. As the story unfolds, she illustrates her words. There's a nice clown who has a cat. The cat is hiding and the clown is mad. She draws the cat and the clown and she doesn't stop talking. This is not the same as telling pictureless stories to her stuffed animals. The pictureless stories disappear the minute she stops speaking. Afterward she can't remember the narratives, and neither can her button-eyed friends. But when she draws her ideas, the illustrations stay on the page permanently.

She brings her picture to Mom and Dad. She tells them the story, pointing to each event in the drawing as she talks. Hours or even weeks later, she can glance at the picture on the refrigerator door and the whole story, or parts of it anyway, will come back to her. By way of a cat and a clown, Debby has discovered the durability of stories when they exist on paper.

A few months later, Debby takes a piece of paper and covers the sheet with squiggles.

Triumphantly, Debby brings the sheet to her mother. She announces that she's written a story and proceeds to "read."

Debby's mother is amused by her daughter's jottings. But she should also be proud. Debby's squiggles signify a new and important stage in her writing development. Earlier Debby used graphic representation—a drawing—to tell her story. The drawing communicates meaning with only a little bit of outside help. But squiggles are different. The squiggles represent words, not images. Right now, Debby thinks that any set of squiggles can represent words. She doesn't realize that only special squiggles, the ones we call letters, have this power.

Before long, Debby figures this out and decides to write a story using her favorite letters.

She hands the paper to her mother and asks, "What did I write?"

Debby covered her page with letters, but she had no story, no words in mind as she did so. The letters were just marks placed on paper. Yet Debby assumes that she has written a story. Stories are, after all, composed of letters. But she can't read, and so, of course, doesn't know what the letters say. Her mom, on the other hand, reads very well. Debby imagines, therefore, that her mom will make sense of the writing and read her story.

The next time Debby writes a story, she tries a different approach—one that shows increased understanding of writing. This time she begins with words in mind. She matches each word with random letters. It's not easy to remember which words she intended. She makes the effort, though, in order to share the story with her parents.

In kindergarten, Debby learns to identify all the letters in the alphabet and to assign one sound to each letter. She enjoys mastering the alphabet because it made her proud and her parents so happy. She is unaware of any additional value in knowing letter sounds, however. Debby, like most young children, does not realize that words can be broken up into smaller parts, namely letter sounds. The word *cat*, for instance, can be split into three sounds: *cuh-ah-tuh*. In general, children don't spontaneously decompose words, even if they know their alphabet. Why should they? *Cat*, the word, has meaning. The isolated sounds do not. When Debby enters first grade, however, direct instruction from her teachers, coupled with her own observations of how people "sound out" words, leads her to a new and very important realization. If she listens carefully, she can actually hear individual sounds within every word. What's more, she can represent those sounds with specific letters. She tries this one day when writing a story about a bear. Slowly and carefully, she says *bear* to herself and smiles as she distinguishes the first sound—buh.

She knows which letter makes the buh sound: it's a *B*. She writes a large *B* on her page. She hears another sound—rrr. She knows that *R* matches this sound. Putting the *B* and the *R* together, Debby writes what she imagines to be *bear*. It looks like this: *BR*. That is not a correct spelling of *bear*. It is an invented spelling. But it is an intelligent invention. It coordinates sounds and letters. Her story is somewhat limited: it consists of the two letters *BR*. Even so, this is a big step forward. Debby has a story in mind, and she has set out to record it using the accepted system for preserving words. Her method is not too accurate but she is on the right track. She now knows that writing a story is not exactly the same as telling a story or drawing a picture.

She is, in fact, a writer at this point. She is the author of *BR*.

By the end of first grade, Debby will write stories that are considerably more complex than *BR*. Single-word stories will become single-sentence stories. Then she will write whole paragraphs. By the end of third grade, she will be the author of several mini-books—each one three to six pages long, with illustrations. In those crucial years, she will learn to write her letters neatly. She will write in print and in script. Her spelling will move inch by inch toward dictionary perfection.

She will become a better storyteller. Her vocabulary and control over language will grow. Her ideas will become more elaborate, her characters more defined. She will develop a literary style—a way of expressing herself—that she can use when writing a creative story about bears or a factual report on volcanoes. She will learn to rewrite and edit her stories in order to express her ideas with greater clarity. By the end of third grade, Debby will manage to express her thoughts on paper without profound difficulty. She will still have a great deal to learn, of course, but she will have made a good start.

Naturally many children have a somewhat harder time, and while the problems they run into are infinite—for writing itself is infinitely difficult—the problems can be summed up in three words: spelling, handwriting, fear. Each of these can present horrendous difficulties for a child, yet each can be overcome, with the right approach.

Spelling

When it comes to spelling, English is a nightmare. There are logical languages, like Spanish, that are phonetically regular. If you can pronounce a Spanish word, you can spell it correctly. Not English. Think of the word *comb*. Shouldn't it be spelled *come* since it rhymes with *home*? Alas, *come* is a word that rhymes with *dumb*. There's that *b* again! You see the problem.

Most children try to memorize the correct spelling of common words. There is no way, however, for a young writer to memorize every word he needs—unless the child severely limits his compositions. Some children do limit themselves that way. They produce narrow little stories such as: "I like cats. I like dogs. I like Mom. I like Dad." Other children try to sound out unknown words as they write, deriving the spelling from the sounds. But that's tricky. Even if you hear every sound, which is difficult enough, assigning appropriate letters is no easy task. When children produce stories based on sounding out words, the results look strange. They may want to write, "My favorite food is spaghetti and tomato sauce." But it comes out, "Mi fvrit fud iz spgte end tumaytow saws."

Many adults consider the "I like" story acceptable, if boring. You can read all the words, dull as they are. The spaghetti lover's story is harder to swallow. Gut reaction may lead parents to believe that stories you can read easily are preferable to a barely decipherable collection of letters.

In this case, though, that gut reaction is not to be trusted. A child who writes with freedom of expression, no matter how peculiar his rendering of words, will develop writing skills more swiftly than a child who crimps his style and limits his ideas for the sake of correct spelling.

The best way to help your child overcome the dreadful burdens that accompany writing in English is to tell him not to worry about spelling as he writes. Encourage your child to sound out unknown words, and when the child comes up with a unique spelling, accept his inventions without hesitation. *Fud* for *food*? Yes, it's acceptable. Many parents are skeptical on hearing this advice. They wonder how their children will ever learn proper spelling. The answer is: word by word and story by story.

Children who write without undue concern for spelling write more words more often than children who are determined to spell with dictionary accuracy. Moreover, children who sound out words invariably learn a great deal about the rules of spelling. It takes time, but by sounding out words children begin to generalize spelling rules for themselves, based on comparing their misspellings with the standard forms. Slowly, they figure out the principles, such as they are, of English spelling, and anything that a child figures out for himself is bound to stay in his memory.

With regard to spelling, then, the best thing a parent can do is not to worry about perfection. Benign patience will be rewarded, for the stumbling child will eventually make the necessary progress. It is far more important to encourage a child to be a fluent writer than a good speller.

Handwriting

Several years ago my grandmother said to me, "It's such a shame that you never learned to write." I was surprised by this statement and reminded her that I was the author of several books. "I know that. I mean your handwriting. It's a disgrace. In my day we learned to write. We had penmanship lessons."

I didn't argue with my grandmother, but I knew that she was 95 percent wrong: penmanship and writing are not synonymous. And making a big to-do over handwriting is, in general, ill-advised. Children who worry over beautiful *p*'s and *q*'s are less likely to write relaxed, flowing prose. Nevertheless, handwriting cannot be ignored. Children must learn to form legible letters. When a child's handwriting is illegible, it is possible that neither he nor anyone else can figure out his words. If that happens, the child's writing progress is in jeopardy. Penmanship is, therefore, still important. But getting a child to write legibly is not always easy to do. Learning to control a pencil is hard for many young children. The multitudinous tiny muscles in a child's hand have to work together in just the right way. And problems don't end once a child's fingers develop the necessary muscle control.

The child has to remember how to form all the lowercase and uppercase letters in the alphabet. The single tiny distinction between *b* and *d* is a plague. There are the little crucial differences between *g*, *q*, and *p*. Worse yet, the letters have to be neat, too. In the face of these many visual and muscular difficulties, a young child has two choices. He can write very slowly and carefully, concentrating on each letter (in which case his handwriting will be beautiful but there will be very few words on the page), or he can concentrate on writing with only the smallest regard for penmanship. His lettering may be a mess, but he will write without inhibition.

Generally speaking, adults should encourage children to sacrifice beautiful letters in favor of a rush of words. You should assure your child that forming graceful letters is a fine thing to do, but getting all his thoughts recorded on the page is finer still.

Fear

When children tell stories, they let loose a stream of words and ideas. But when they write, they get self-conscious. Just like adult writers facing the blank page, children wonder if their ideas are interesting, their stories dynamic, their writing style clear. To express their thoughts on the page seems an impossible task. Some children find the challenge paralyzing. They have writer's block even before they have learned to write.

What can adults do to help in such a situation? Give the child a thousand opportunities to write. It's not necessary for children to compose full-length stories. Youngsters can write brief lists and scribble stray thoughts. Anything they write will do some good— as long as they get a few words down on paper. The more children write, the less self-conscious they become. Words flow, skills grow. In writing, as in everything else, practice makes perfect. Less than perfect is acceptable, too.

But how to get your child to do the correct amount of practice? How to overcome the stumbling blocks of spelling, handwriting, and fear? Here is where games come in.

Parents and Writing

You, as a parent, have a special role in your child's educational development. All the evidence suggests that when parents are active participants in a child's education, the child reaps tremendous benefits. But what does participation mean? It doesn't mean taking the place of a classroom teacher. You shouldn't try to introduce difficult new topics to your child, and, by and large, you shouldn't drill the child. Instead, participating means visiting school, supervising homework, and expressing concerned interest in your child's academic progress. It means getting your child involved in academic tasks as part of everyday life. It means making your home an intellectually exciting place. And one way to do that is to play games that have a sound educational purpose.

Parents play games with children all the time. Why not, then, pick games that, in addition to being fun, will surreptitiously provide a bit of beneficial instruction? Using the proper game, you can help your child practice, and eventually master, almost any skill needed for writing. Games give children the opportunity to play with spelling and grammar the way they play with blocks and dolls. Better yet, you can help your child master the greatest of all skills: the skill of taking pleasure in learning new and challenging things.

The activities in *Games for Writing* don't require extensive equipment, nor are they time-consuming. In *Games for Writing* you will find meaningful ways to amuse your child while standing on a supermarket line or waiting for take-out at your favorite Chinese restaurant. There are games that will take up the minutes before a favorite TV show comes on the air. There are games that may replace TV altogether on some winter evenings. There are silly games, competitive games, cooperative games, artistic games, and dice games. The games fit comfortably into the lives of busy children and even busier parents. The games are fun and beneficial both for children who are struggling with writing and for those who write with unencumbered ease.

There are some points you should keep in mind while playing these games with your children. First and foremost, have fun. I've tested each and every one of these games with children. To merit entry in the book, a game had to be fun for several different young players. But I don't expect every game to delight every child, and you shouldn't imagine that your child will like all of the games, either. Some of the games will be fun for you, the grown-up, and others will be a bore. There are many games in *Games for Writing*. So if you don't enjoy a particular activity, just flip through the pages until you find one more to your liking.

In the course of playing, you will surely see your child make mistakes. You will see misspelled words, reversed *b*'s and *d*'s, unique uses of capital and lowercase letters. Don't worry about these problems. Just keep playing. Trust that given time, help in school, and exposure to your own correct usage, your child will learn. If you fuss about spelling or handwriting—outside of a spelling or handwriting game, that is—you will bring the fun to a halt. Your child won't want to play anymore. Will that help him to spell more proficiently or write more legibly? It will not. So let the mistakes pass.

Do you remember when your child was learning to talk? You were amused by his grammatical errors and idiosyncratic vocabulary. You didn't correct him. You sensed that a noncritical approach was the right one. It is the right approach now, too.

Using *Games for Writing*

There are five parts to *Games for Writing*. Part One, "Just for Starters," has eleven activities that are designed to ease kindergarteners and first-graders into writing. Playing the games in Part One, children can learn to control their pencils and produce properly formed letters. They can learn to tell well-organized tales instead of semicoherent stories. Best of all, children don't need to know much about writing to play these games, not even how to spell their own names. Yet the games will help young children develop notions about writing and specific skills that are crucial for success in learning how to write.

Young writers tend to be nervous writers. They find it hard to pick suitable topics. It's difficult for them to think of the right words. It's tedious getting words down on paper. There are games and activities, however, that can reduce these difficulties. I've compiled sixteen of these activities in Part Two. I call these activities stress busters. To be a stress buster, a writing activity must meet two criteria. First, it should be a bit silly. Ideally, a child engaged in writing a stress buster will find himself giggling now and again. There's nothing better than a touch of laughter to calm a child's fears. Second, it should take very little time to complete. A stress buster should limit the writing demands on a child without limiting his creativity or imagination.

Part Three is called "Bugaboos—Spelling, Handwriting, and Grammar." Here you will find nine playful ways to help your child improve his spelling, beautify his handwriting, and increase his understanding of English grammar.

The activities in Part Four, "Writing with Style," will help children write sophisticated stories. After playing these games, children will find it easy to create unusual fictional characters. They will develop mature notions of story structure and learn to pick the right words to express their ideas.

When you have time to take on longer writing projects, you can find them in Part Five, "Made with Pride." Some of the activities in this section will require about a half-hour or so to complete. Others will involve several sessions of work (and play) over many weeks.

How should you select activities? Browse through the book. Look for games that seem both appealing and suited to your child's age and ability. Each game is labeled by grade level, which should help you make a choice. If you want to play a game designated for a first-grader with a third-grade youngster, that's perfectly fine. The reverse, however, is not. To play a third-grade game with a first-grader is a sure way to frustrate the child, which would be counterproductive. By and large, though, if you pick the wrong game, no harm will be done. Your child will be bored, and you will know instantly that the game is not a hit. You may find, though, that January's failed game may be June's activity of the month. Children change and their tastes change, too. When you pick a game that your child likes, you may find yourself playing the game over and over. That's fine, too. Whatever you do, keep in mind your main purpose for playing: to increase your child's pleasure in writing. You want your child to feel comfortable when he confronts a blank sheet of paper. You want him to feel confident of his abilities as a writer. So be free with compliments. Congratulate your child on his ideas and accomplishments. Don't worry about his mistakes. If you let your child know that you are proud of his efforts and delighted with the risks he is taking, you will help him to enjoy writing and take pride in his own achievements.

Your part in all this is quite easy. Just call your child to your side, pick a game, and begin.

PART ONE
JUST FOR STARTERS

What was your child's first word? Was it *Dada* or *Mama*? That special word was a milestone in your child's life. But before the milestone came a thousand little steps. There was the first gurgle. There were the hours your child spent staring uncomprehendingly at you while you talked. There were hums and squawks of every kind, each of which was a crucial new experiment in making sounds. Only after taking every one of these tiny steps did your child produce his miraculous first venture into the world of verbal expression: "Dada." "Mama."

Writing, too, requires a thousand steps before the first word ever gets written down. And just as you helped your child through the steps that led to speech, you can help with the thousand steps that lead to writing. You can start by playing one of the eleven games in this section. The games are designed for children in kindergarten and first grade. Each game might not seem like much, but each one helps the child master a tiny skill, and the skills add up. There is, for instance, the skill of scribbling. Imagine a child scribbling with a pencil while telling a story. Ask the child what he's doing and he will answer, "I'm writing." You smile indulgently and leave him to his fantasy play. But he isn't merely fantasizing. He is engaged in one of the genuine aspects of writing, more or less the way an infant who engages in baby prattle is taking one of the steps that lead to speech.

The child who engages in scribble writing is experimenting with a major new idea. He is using graphic forms to express his thoughts. He is giving his words a physical reality on the page. The notion that you can give words a permanent home by using a pencil and paper is a giant step in a child's thinking. Sure, the permanent home is only a scribble, but the evolution from inde-cipherable scribbles to proper letters is something that will come in time.

All babies prattle, but not all young children scribble while telling stories. If your child doesn't do it spontaneously, try playing WRIBBLING, the first game in this section.

Naturally, a child can't start scribbling unless he can control his pencil, and that can be difficult for young children. It's hard to grip a pencil properly and keep the lines moving in the intended direction. Two games in this chapter, THREE-COLOR ROAD RACE and OBSTACLE COURSE, help children command those sticks of wood and graphite.

JUST WHAT I SAID will help your child tell his left side from his right. It's important for young children to become familiar with these directions. In Chinese the writing goes from top to bottom, and in Hebrew from right to left. But in English we write from left to right. We write that way all the time—not just sometimes, as many children like to believe. It takes considerable awareness of right and left before children can get this basic fact of writing lodged in their young minds.

Some of the best writing activities for young children don't involve paper or pencil at all. How can that be? To make up a story and to write it down are not the same thing, yet both are components of what we call writing. Consider Homer, the blind poet of Ancient Greece. He recited; others wrote down the words. When it comes to telling stories, every child is a little Homer. Unfortunately, little Homers tend to meander confusedly in their storytelling. Three games in this section, CATCH MY SILLY, STORY MAPS, and READ ALOUD PLUS, encourage children to make up tales with a strong story line.

It's a good idea to let your child dictate stories to an experienced writer such as yourself. When you do so, your child gets to see his words on paper. That's exciting. Better yet, you can read his stories over and over again. Why, that makes his stories just like tales in books. Two games here, SAY IT WITH PICTURES and WRITE IT FOR ME, help you give your child this valuable experience.

The final two activities help children learn to recognize and form letters correctly—while eating popcorn and baking pretzels.

Will all eleven games appeal to your child? Probably not. Will one or another game appeal? In all likelihood, yes. Skim through this section. If an activity looks amusing, pick a quiet moment and play. Some games will be so successful, you'll want to divert yourselves with them again and again. Others may be great—once—but you won't care to play a second round. A few games may need a bit of adjusting before they are perfectly tailored for use in your house. There is one, and only one, unalterable rule about the games: you and your child must enjoy the time you spend playing them. If a game seems like work, it isn't working.

F

ive-year-old Joey loved making up stories. He had an amazing supply of tales to tell. He knew how to develop a plot, create characters, and evoke a variety of emotions for an eager audience of family, friends, and teachers. But he didn't know how to get his stories down on paper.

He was too young to be taught to write in any conventional sense. Even so, there were two ways to encourage him to associate his storytelling with writing on the page. One way was for him to dictate his stories to me, and for me to write them down. To take dictation from a young writer is always a good idea. It helps a child see how spoken words get written on a page, and how written words stay exactly where you put them, whereas spoken words evaporate at once.

There was another way to encourage Joey. That was to inspire him to write for himself by means of his own invented system. His system didn't include letters as we think of them. Letters were beyond his capability. But there was no reason for him not to write with his nonsensical loops, zigs, and zags.

Joey's first zigzag writing happened accidentally. We were play-acting a story about a pizza parlor that delivers pizza pies exclusively to superheroes. We had just gotten a call from Spiderman. He was in desperate need of a pepperoni and mushroom pizza. I grabbed a piece of paper and said, "Quick, Joey, write the order while I heat the oven."

"I can't write," he protested.

"Well, maybe you can't write with letters, but you can write like this," I said as I scrawled squiggles on a paper.

Joey looked at me and smiled, "Peggy, you're scribbling."

"No I'm not. I'm *wribbling*. Wribbling is part scribble and part

GRADES

kindergarten and first

MATERIALS

paper
pencil

writing. It can be our own special way of taking pizza orders. Do you think you can wribble Spiderman's order?"

"I think so," he said, and he began wribbling. When he was done, he handed me the sheet.

"Great, it says pepperoni and mushrooms. Thank goodness you wrote it down. I almost made pepper and mustard by mistake."

"Spiderman would be mad," Joey replied.

Over the next several weeks, Joey and I engaged in a considerable amount of playacting. We ran an auto repair shop. I shouted orders like, "Fix the fender!" And Joey wribbled something down on paper and handed it to me. We playacted a veterinarian clinic. "This dog is sick! He needs medicine!" I said. Joey wribbled a prescription. "This cat has a broken tail. He needs a cast. Order some plaster," I said. Joey wribbled a supply order. We playacted a toy store. "We must have a hundred more toy trucks by Saturday. Write a purchase order." Joey wribbled a few lines on a piece of paper. Using several sheets of paper, we created our own toy catalogue. Each bit of play called for WRIBBLING.

Wribbling pizza orders and toy catalogues may not be the most traditional way to teach beginning writing, but it's easy, it's fun, and it works. Joey had always liked telling stories. Now he liked to tell stories and scribble with a pencil at the same time. He had taken a step toward writing—a tiny step, but a necessary one.

6

THREE-COLOR ROAD RACE

*A*nyone who has watched a young child pick up a pencil and start to draw knows how difficult this task can be. We aren't born knowing how to hold a pencil or how to control a pencil line. Before we can draw all the straight and curved lines that constitute our horribly complicated written alphabet, we have to learn how to handle those little graphite sticks. Your child can learn in an entertaining way when you start a THREE-COLOR ROAD RACE.

To play, you need two blank sheets of paper. On one sheet, draw a road across the top of the page. The road might look like this:

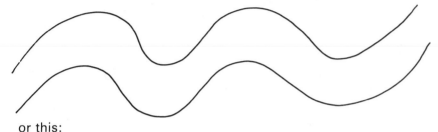

or this:

or this:

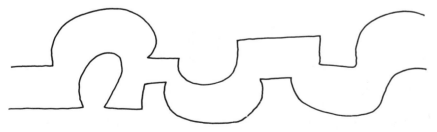

Then draw a more-or-less identical road on the top of the second sheet.

GRADES

kindergarten and first

MATERIALS

blank paper
pen
six different colored pencils

Now you and your child should each select three colored pencils. When you're both facing your own roads with sharp pencils at hand, call out, "Get ready! Get set! GO!" On the word *Go*, grab one of your pencils and, as fast as you can, draw a line from the left side to the right side of the road.

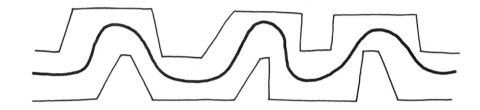

You must not touch the edge lines. If you do, you have to return to the beginning of the road and start your trip again. When you reach the end, pick up a second pencil. Now draw a second line, from left to right, along the road. Again, you mustn't touch the edge lines. You don't need to worry, though, if you overlap your first colored line. When you're done, grab your third color and zoom off down the road one more time. When your third line arrives at the end of the road, shout, "STOP!"

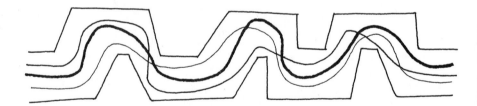

As you work, your child will be drawing three colorful lines across his own road. He might manage the job and shout, "Stop!" before you do. If he does, he wins the game. Maybe, if you ask sweetly, your child will agree to play again. A new game gives you another chance to win, and it gives your child another chance to perfect his pencil grip and learn to control his pencil line.

What if your child keeps running off the road? No problem. Just widen the road.

Nancy loved playing OBSTACLE COURSE. It's true that she had trouble requesting the game. "Can we play oppical?" she used to ask. But that was good enough. OBSTACLE COURSE is not a pronunciation game; it's a pencil game. It helped Nancy learn to hold a pencil correctly and to control its movement across a page. Soon enough she would have to learn to write the fifty-two upper- and lowercase letters of our alphabet, so it was a good idea to begin with pencil control.

Before we started the game, I needed a blank sheet of paper and a pencil. I drew a box on the upper-left-hand side of the paper and labeled it HOME. I drew a box labeled PARK on the bottom-right-hand corner of the page. Finally, I sketched many lines jutting this way and that way across the page. I called these "obstacles."

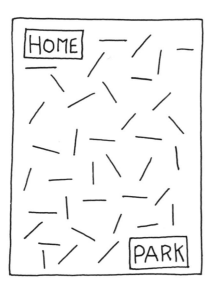

The object of the game is to draw a path from HOME to PARK without touching any obstacles. If Nancy could successfully negotiate her way, she won. If she couldn't, she lost.

When Nancy traversed this OBSTACLE COURSE, she worked slowly and carefully. She twisted right and turned left, avoiding pitfall after pitfall. A few times she lifted her pencil off the page, shook out her hand, and then went back to work. As she neared

GRADES
kindergarten and first

MATERIALS
paper
pencil

her goal, she started humming. When she reached the park, we both shouted, "Hooray!"

Victory felt so good, Nancy wanted to play again. The more she played, the more control she had over her pencil. That was victory for me. I knew that if Nancy could get safely from HOME to PARK she would eventually be able to get around the angles of a capital *E* or the curves of a capital *B.*

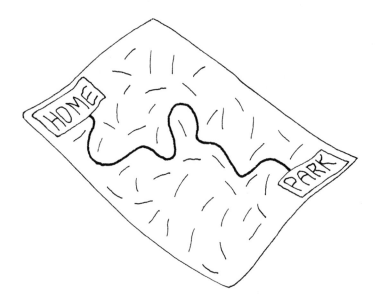

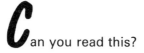 **C**an you read this?

GRADES

kindergarten and first

MATERIALS

a quarter
masking tape
pen

It says (starting from the bottom) "My cat likes to play." It's one of Jesse's early kindergarten stories. Jesse knew a great deal about writing for such a young child. He knew how to write a sentence. He knew how to spell several words. But he did not know that words on a page must begin in a certain spot, and go from there in a certain direction, line by line, from top to bottom.

There's nothing very surprising in Jesse's failure to know these points. When he sits down to draw a picture with a pencil and paper, he never worries about starting at the top or moving from left to right, and he is correct not to worry. How was he to know that writing is different from drawing? In his entire young life it had never been necessary to distinguish left from right. Unfortunately, when you write words, direction does make a difference. So it was time, as I could see from Jesse's creative way of writing "My cat likes to play," for him to learn about left and right. Therefore, I introduced him to JUST WHAT I SAID.

Before the game began, I took a quarter and taped a bit of masking tape over the top and bottom of the coin. I wrote a *P*, for Peggy, on one side and a *J*, for Jesse, on the reverse side.

I handed the coin to Jesse and told him to toss it in the air. If the quarter landed on the table with the *P* side facing up, I got to order Jesse around and he had to do JUST WHAT I SAID. I could tell him to touch his left big toe with his right elbow. I could tell him to hop all the way around the room on his left foot. I might order him to wiggle his left thumb and pinkie—while trying to keep his other fingers absolutely still. I might insist he wave his right hand in the air while turning round and round in a circle. I could concoct any order at all—as long as it had a left or a right in it. If the coin landed with the *J* side facing up, Jesse got to invent a left or right order for me to obey. Jesse didn't care which letter landed facing us. He liked giving orders, and he liked taking them, too.

I didn't expect Jesse to memorize left and right simply by playing this game. I merely wanted him to focus his attention on these directions. Soon he would realize that, in books, writing always goes from left to right. Initially he might memorize this fact but in time he would absorb it so deeply he would no longer need to remember it—any more than he needs to remember his name.

I flipped the coin first, and since it landed with the *P* up, I got to order him to do something involving left or right.

"Hop on your left foot, Jesse," I said.

And he did.

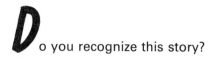

Do you recognize this story?

Once upon a time there is a witch and the girl and boy they're lost in the woods. And the witch wants to eat the boy. The witch has a candy house. And they get there because a bird eats the bread so they don't go home. The witch tries to get them, but they trick her and push her in the oven.

What is the story? It's "Hansel and Gretel," as told by Lucy, a lively five-year-old. Lucy included all the major events, though she did reorder a few things in the process.

That is typical of the young storyteller. The young child tells the most important parts first. The witch is important. And almost getting eaten is *very* important. So Lucy begins with these harrowing moments. A young child doesn't see any advantage to telling a story sequentially. The result? Narrative chaos. As children get older, they appreciate the importance of telling stories in chronological order. They try to tell their tales in standard sequence. Even to make the effort is a significant milepost in a child's literary development. But getting things in order is hard to do.

I used a game called CATCH MY SILLY to speed the learning process for Lucy. The game required me to make up stories. Sometimes I told true stories about my week. I recounted a shopping expedition or a trip to the zoo. Other times I made up adventures starring a little girl named Lucy. I let my imagination fly and invented fantasies about magic lands, friendly sorcerers, and tricky dragons.

What makes a CATCH MY SILLY story special? A sprinkling of sillies. Read this one and you'll get the idea.

Mark woke up early one Saturday. Today was special. Today he'd get a new bike. He jumped into bed and rushed to get dressed. After he put on his shoes, he put on his socks. He rushed downstairs for dinner. His mom and dad were still asleep. So Mark decided to fix his own meal. He closed the refrigerator door and took out the milk. Then he took a box of cereal.

Did you catch the sillies? There are five of them. Would Mark really wake up and jump into bed? No, no, that's silly. Would he put on his shoes and then his socks? No, no, that's silly. Did you enjoy catching sillies? Lucy did. She loved shouting, "NO! NO! THAT'S SILLY!" every time she recognized a bit of story confusion.

I told the story slowly and let a moment lapse after each sentence. Even so, Lucy did miss some of the sillies. What did I do then? Nothing. I just went on talking. Why didn't I challenge Lucy? I wanted her to feel 100 percent effective at this game. Correcting her, therefore, would have been counterproductive.

Every silly I provided for Lucy had a serious intent. Each one helped her think about the logical quality of a good story. To go to bed as soon as you wake up is not logical. To have dinner in the morning is not logical. Nor is it logical to close the refrigerator door before getting out the milk.

Eventually Lucy realized that ordering events correctly is important to any story. In time, her own stories began unfolding in chronological fashion. When things did get jumbled, Lucy noticed. She tried to set matters right. She wasn't always successful, but that didn't worry me. Her effort showed that she had reached a new stage in understanding stories.

It's fairly easy to make up silly tales, but you might not always be in the creative mood. At such a time, read one of the following stories to your child. After each story you will see a number telling how many sillies I've planted. Challenge your child to find the sillies or work together to unearth them. Feel free to use some of the silly ideas here when you do make up your own tales.

Tony came home from school Thursday afternoon. He had a snack and got ready to do his homework. He put his school books in his book bag, sat at his desk, and got to work. "Tomorrow is Monday," he said to himself. "That means I have a spelling test." He opened his math book, so he could study his spelling list. After he finished his homework he drew a picture of his dog to give his mom as a present. "I'll give it to her before she comes home from work," he thought. Tony asked his babysitter if she wanted to play checkers. They put away the board and started to play. Soon it was time for breakfast. Tony helped his babysitter make hamburgers, French fries, and broccoli. Tony's mom came home just as the hamburgers were ready to put under the oven. Tony, his mom, and his babysitter ate a yummy dinner of hot dogs, French fries, and broccoli.

(There are eight sillies in this story.)

★

Melissa loved dinosaurs. She had ten books about the little animals on her bookshelf. In a bookstore she saw a brand-new dinosaur book. She wanted it. The clothing-store clerk said the book cost two dollars. Melissa's mom gave her the money. Melissa paid for the book and then left it in the store. When she got home she took the book to the living room. Her mom read it to her on the kitchen sofa. It was the best book about dinosaurs Melissa ever heard. She learned new facts about rabbits. She put the book on her shelf.

Now she had five dinosaur books. Melissa still had lots of questions about dinosaurs. She wondered what they liked to eat. She wondered if they slept standing up or lying down. She didn't want to find the answers. Her mother helped her sing a letter to a dinosaur expert. After a week, the dinosaur expert wrote back to Molly. He answered all her questions and he invited her to visit him at his dinosaur museum. Me-

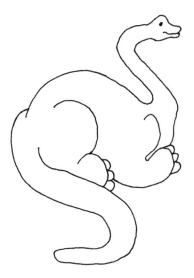

Catch My Silly

lissa went to the museum. The dinosaur expert showed her lots of sailboats. It was a great day.

(There are ten sillies in this story.)

★

Tom was a brave knight, but he was very clumsy. When Tom got on his horse, he always fell up. One day, he got a letter from the queen. He closed the envelope, put away the letter, and started to read. "Please capture the huge dragon in the mountains. She is a scary dragon and everyone likes her."

Tom called for his horse. He started to ride away from the mountains. On the way, he saw a baby dragon lost in the woods.

"Help me," said the baby.

"I will," said Tom.

He rode away on his horse and then he gently picked up the baby. He took the baby into the mountains. He found the dragon's cave. Inside the cave he heard the mother dragon crying, "Where is my baby?"

Tom climbed off his horse. He put his sword into his belt just in case the dragon attacked. Then he carried the baby outside the cave. The mother dragon was so happy to see her baby, she gave the knight a big kiss.

Tom said, "Please come and live with me. You are scaring people in the mountains. But you don't scare me. I like you."

And so the dragon unpacked all of her things and went with Tom back to his house. The mother dragon, the baby dragon, and Tom lived happily ever after.

(There are nine sillies in this story.)

Like most five-year-olds, Janet loved making up stories. Given the slightest encouragement, she would tell tales of giants, elves, and flying princesses. Her stories were fanciful and exciting, but garbled. Her plots veered wildly from alligator attacks to Ferris wheel rides. There was almost never a connection between one bit of narrative and the next.

I didn't want to inhibit Janet's style. I did, however, want to help her invent more coherent stories. For this to happen, Janet needed a co-writer, someone who would approve some ideas and nix others. It would have been wrong to barge in on her freewheeling tales, but I could propose a game in which sharing a story with me would be perfectly natural. STORY MAP is just such a game. Before starting the joint story, though, you must spend about ten minutes making a STORY MAP. A STORY MAP begins with a blank sheet of paper or oaktag. A big sheet is best, at least 14″ × 17″. On this sheet you should design an imaginary neighborhood. Something like this:

Or this:

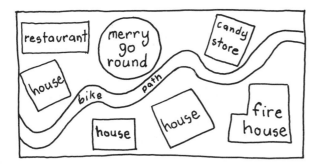

GRADES

kindergarten and first

MATERIALS

a large sheet of blank paper or oaktag (at least 14″ × 17″)
crayons or colored markers
small toy figures

The very first story map that I made with Janet looked like this:

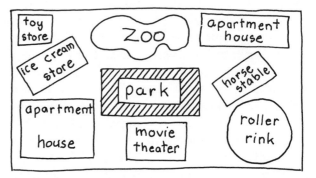

How did we create the map? I presented Janet with a sheet of oaktag and said, "Last night I had an idea. I decided we would create our own imaginary world right here on paper."

Janet looked perplexed but interested. I said, "What should we include? An apartment house? A supermarket? A playground? I know, let's begin with a park. Now, where should we put it?"

Before I could offer a suggestion, Janet shouted, "Here!" and pointed to the middle of the page.

"That's a fine spot," I said. I outlined a rectangular park. Together Janet and I colored the area green. I labeled the spot.

Now that Janet had the idea, she became a mapmaker. She instructed me to draw a toy store, an ice cream store, a movie theater, a zoo, a roller rink, two apartment buildings, and a horse stable. It was an interesting neighborhood.

Next we turned our attention to people. We needed to populate our imaginary world. With this in mind, I pulled out a shoe box full of tiny toys—miniature animals, dolls, cars, people, and creatures. Janet selected her favorite—a dainty troll with fluorescent hair—to use for her story character. I picked an itsy-bitsy black cat.

If you don't have tiny toys in your house, you can create homemade story characters. Just get an index card and cut it in fourths. Bend each piece in half so it stands like a tent.

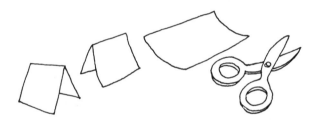

Draw a small person or animal on one side. If you don't want to draw, pull out your child's sticker collection, select two lively pictures, and stick them on the cards.

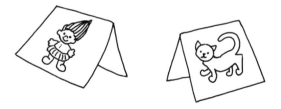

Of course, characters need names. Janet christened her troll Amelia. I named my cat Hortense. I declared Hortense to be a talking cat and began speaking for her.

"It's such a lovely day, Amelia, let's go for a walk in the park."

Janet didn't have any problems entering the story. "Okay, let's go," she said. And we maneuvered the troll and the cat across the story map toward the park.

On the way, I stopped and exclaimed, "Look, an ice cream store! Can we get some ice cream?"

Amelia agreed. So we went into the store. I became the sales clerk and handed Hortense and Amelia pretend vanilla cones. Then cat and troll continued strolling.

When we reached the park, Janet let loose a flurry of story suggestions.

"I know," she began. "There's a witch in the park, okay? And it's Amelia's birthday and the guests are coming. But it rains. And then wild animals escape from the zoo. You know, lions and tigers . . ."

"What great ideas, Janet," I said. "Let's pick just one for now, though. Do you want a witch, or a birthday party, or escaping tigers?"

It was a hard choice. Janet settled on the birthday party and we went on with the story.

For the most part, our tale progressed in a fine manner. Occasionally, though, Janet had odd leaps of fancy. Witches suddenly appeared accompanied by giant ants. Thunderstorms produced earthquakes, which led to attacks by snowmen. When confusion took over, I gently trimmed down the plot. I gave Janet choices. I made connections between past events and future occurrences. It was easy to do this without dampening Janet's enthusiasm. I just had to give her guidance without criticizing her ideas. I never said, "That doesn't make sense." Instead I said, "I like the thunderstorm and the earthquake, but let's not worry about the snowman." And so the story proceeded, imaginatively but not illogically.

When we finished the story, we put the map away on a bookshelf. The next time we played STORY MAPS, we could either take out this map or make a new one. If the spirit moved us, we could design a fantasy map complete with a castle, an enchanted forest, a glass mountain, or a magic waterfall. Imagine the stories we could imagine then!

Here are some story-map suggestions. Use them if you want, or forget them.

An outer-space map with planets, comets, and space stations.

A spooky map with a haunted house, a witch's cave, and a monster's castle.

An amusement park with a roller coaster ride, a Ferris wheel, a carousel, and a hot dog and cotton candy stand.

A shopping mall with a bookstore, a toy store, a pizza parlor, a bank, and a post office.

READ ALOUD PLUS

*O*ne of the best possible things you can do for your child is to read aloud. Reading aloud teaches a child to enjoy stories, to expand his imagination, and eventually to do his own reading, which is immensely important. But reading aloud has one further grand virtue: it permits you and your child to engage in a bit of critical commentary. "Ah, yes," you might say, pushing the book away for a brief second, "I like the part about the beanstalk. Don't you?"

In that way you can encourage your child to get more deeply involved. The two of you (or the three of you, or ten of you) can share thoughts about the characters and the story and the setting. It's always good to engage in a little prediction, "What do you think will happen next?"

When your child predicts an upcoming scene or event, he is, in fact, composing the next part of the tale. He may have different plot ideas from the author. That is perfectly fine. Predicting what will happen next is not a test. It is a way of enjoying the story, and it is a way of encouraging a child to expand his understanding of story plots. It is a way of getting a child to think the way a writer thinks.

When you read longer books that might take several nights to complete, extend your talk. Over dinner, you might want to discuss diet plans for Pooh or consider the best games to play with Tigger.

Your child will be happy to engage in such discussion, and the happier he is, the more he will appreciate books, stories, and writing.

SAY IT WITH PICTURES

*B*rett was a first-grader who had no interest in writing or reading. But he did like looking at nature magazines. He was a fan of cute furry animals. This, I figured, was an opening into the world of writing. I suggested that he cut out pictures of animals so that we could use them to make a special collage.

"What's a collage?" Brett asked.

"A collage is a group of pictures and drawings that you paste on a sheet of paper. Collages are pretty to look at, if you pick good pictures and arrange them in a nice way."

"I can pick good pictures," Brett said. "I want lots of animals."

"Well, then, let's start hunting. While we search for pictures, though, we also need to hunt for words. The words should tell about the pictures. That way we'll have a word-and-picture collage," I said.

"But I can't read," Brett complained.

"That's okay. I'll look for good words and read them to you. If I read a word you like, we'll cut it out. And if you think of a good word—one that you'd like to be part of the collage but we can't find in the magazine—tell me and I'll write it for you."

"Okay," Brett replied.

We turned to the pile of nature magazines and scrutinized the pages. We found a kitten, a raccoon, a bear cub, a chipmunk, a deer, and a big-eyed, irresistibly cute baby bat. We found good words, too: *baby*, *fur*, *wild*, *snuggle*, *camouflage*, *kitten*, *raccoon*, and *chipmunk.*

"I can think of other words, but I don't see them in the magazines," I said.

"Like what?" Brett asked.

"Like *soft* and *charming*," I said. "Can you think of other words to describe our great furry pictures?"

Brett suggested *cute* and the phrase *scary to see.*

"I love those words. I'm going to write them on slips of paper so we can add them to the collage," I said.

I held up a large sheet of oaktag. "Now we glue the pictures and words on the oaktag. We make it as beautiful as we can," I said.

Brett and I fiddled with a few of the pictures, trying them here

GRADES

kindergarten and first

MATERIALS

**oaktag or poster board
glue
colored markers
magazines
paper
scissors
pencil**

and there. We snipped off a bit of the kitten to make it fit exactly where we wanted. With a little scissoring and pasting, we covered the oaktag.

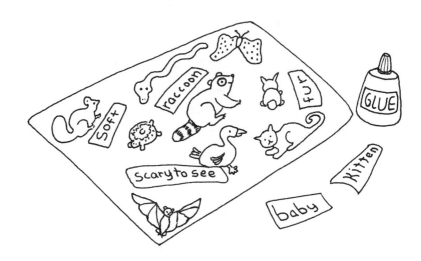

Brett wanted to make another collage right away. He was actually eager to put words on paper, which, for him, was a fairly amazing development. True, he was gluing and not writing these words. But without knowing that he had done so, he had already mastered the hitherto elusive basic concept that words on paper can articulate an exciting vision of life—in his case, an appreciation of furry animals.

If you think a collage will give your child a promising start in writing, I advise you to collect picture magazines. Your child may not be a great animal lover. He may prefer sports, boats, flowers, or monsters. Dinosaurs may delight him. With a little effort, you can find pictures for virtually any interest your child may develop. Let's say your child wants to make a sports collage. You don't have to collect the pictures all at once. Instead, get a large envelope and label it "Cutouts for Sports Collage." You and your child can fill it with interesting words and images. On Saturday, cut out a photo from *Sports Illustrated.* Tuesday, snip an action shot from the newspaper. Next week, cut out a few words from a football article in *Newsweek.* When your envelope is stuffed, start designing your collage. Trim a few pictures, smear some words with paste, and soon you'll have a collage you can proudly hang on your wall.

WRITE IT FOR ME

At the age of four, little George Orwell dictated a poem to his mom. The great literary critic Edmund Wilson began his writing career by dictating stories to his admiring aunt. The child as tiny author dictating precious words to an adoring adult is, I suspect, a scene that takes place at the start of many famous writers' luminous careers.

Over the years, I have taken such dictation from dozens of budding writers, and in every case I have been pleased with the results. They dictate; I scribble down what they say; and by the end, they have established a relation between themselves and words on paper. And they are pleased with themselves, as they should be.

Taking dictation from a child is a very simple activity. You can record your child's stories and poems in the Orwell-Wilson tradition. Or you can take less formal dictations. You can help a child write KEEP OUT—AND THAT MEANS YOU signs, a written request for a later bedtime, thank-you cards to the tooth fairy, and labels for elaborate block buildings.

You can help your child add items to your weekly grocery list, write lists of complaints to an annoying older sister, and compose a birthday card for a special uncle. Your child will be the author of all these works, even without doing the physical work of writing. And, as Mother Orwell or Aunt Wilson could confirm, you never know where such writing will lead.

POPCORN WRITING

Why not try something untraditional with your next bowl of popcorn? Instead of eating it, use the kernels to help your child recognize and form the letters of the alphabet.

That's what I did with Jonathan, who is, in fact, the inventor of this game. Jonathan was the younger brother of one of my students. When he started kindergarten, he declared he wanted to work with me, just as his big brother had. His mother thought this was a good idea, too, especially since he was exhibiting a lot of anxiety over school. So we started working together once a week.

Jonathan came to my office after school. I always had a snack ready for him, which on one occasion happened to be popcorn. The bowl was on the table so Jonathan could nibble while we worked.

Our first lesson of the day concerned the alphabet. Jonathan could read almost all the letters. He knew how to form most of the uppercase letters plus a few of the lowercase ones. Sometimes his letters flipped, turning J into ꓩ and R into Я

These reversals didn't bother me. I knew that with practice he would, in time, realign his letters. My job, then, was to give Jonathan a chance to practice. After Jonathan was settled in his chair, I wrote a large-scale *J* on a sheet of paper.

I wanted Jonathan to pick up his pencil and trace over the *J.* But he had a different idea. Giggling, he grabbed a handful of popcorn and dropped the kernels one by one on the paper.

"Jonathan," I said, "it looks like you want to write with popcorn today."

Jonathan spotted an opportunity for fun. "Can we?" he asked.

"It's a great idea," I said. "All we need is glue to stick the popcorn on the letters."

GRADES

kindergarten and first

MATERIALS

a bowl of unbuttered popcorn
paper
pencil
glue

Before getting the glue, I separated the popcorn into two bowls. One bowl was for eating, the other for writing.

I handed a container of glue to Jonathan. He dribbled a sticky ribbon across the oversized *J.*

The moment the *J* was covered, he pressed popcorn in the glue. Then he gazed with delight on his 3-D popcorn letter.

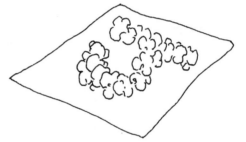

A single letter wouldn't do. Jonathan wanted to write more. He demanded to write. So I took another sheet of paper and drew a jumbo *R.* Jonathan traced it with glue and popcorn. We continued writing letters until we had munched or glued every kernel and the bowls were empty.

It had been a grand day. Jonathan had spent some very useful time contemplating the shapes of *J, R,* and several other letters, and it had been very little work for me. The hard part was mostly being sure that no one made a snack out of any glue-covered popcorn.

Better even than the popcorn approach to writing is the pretzel approach. It's surprisingly easy to cook a batch of homemade soft chewy pretzels, and when you do, you can certainly twist them in the classic form:

But it's vastly more fun and far more interesting to twist the all-accepting dough into alphabet shapes.

GRADES

kindergarten and first

MATERIALS

refrigerated French bread dough
coarse salt
one egg
baking tray
butter or margarine to grease the tray

To make pretzels, all you need is an egg, some coarse salt (sometimes called kosher salt), butter or margarine, and a package of ready-made French bread dough. You can find this dough in the refrigerator section of most supermarkets.

Start by breaking off a small piece of the dough and rolling it into a long snake shape.

Twist and turn the snake until you've formed your favorite letter. You can sprinkle a bit of flour on the dough if it gets too sticky. And you can add extra dough if you need it to finish a letter.

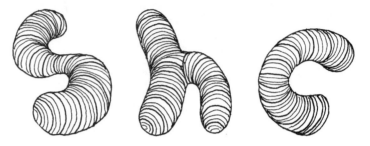

When the pretzel letter is ready, put it on the greased baking tray. Then make a new letter. With enough letters, you can spell words.

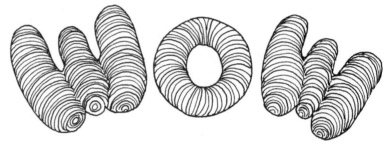

Crack open an egg and separate out the white. Stir the egg white together with a single tablespoon of water. Brush each letter with the egg white. Then sprinkle the pretzels with coarse salt. Bake the pretzel letters at 350 degrees for fifteen to twenty minutes. By then they should be golden brown.

When your letters cool, it's time to eat. The pretzels are excellent when warm and quite delicious at room temperature. If you're from Philadelphia, you know how fine they taste spread with mustard. Before you sink your teeth into the chewy delights, though, consider the educational rationale of this very sensible activity. It is the same reasoning that you will find in the previous activity, POP-CORN WRITING. It is based on the principle that, just as humankind wrote with a stylus on clay before applying ink to parchment with a quill, there is no reason why, in the immediate history of your own family, you cannot write with pretzels on a baking tray. And this activity has a splendid side benefit: after you have formed the letters and contemplated them, you can eat your own words.

PART TWO
STRESS BUSTERS

Some children—a lucky handful—enter first grade already set to start writing. Give these children a sheet of paper and, almost without hesitating, they will scribble sentences on the page. They will very likely use nonsensical letter combinations. They may write "SWSUM" in the belief that it means "I like school."

But no matter. If teachers applaud these early efforts, children who come to first grade with that ability will easily develop their writing skills. In the beginning, these children may seem oblivious to standard spelling. But so long as they believe they are writing, they will go on doing it, and the more they go on, the more they will notice and learn. After several weeks of such composition, these lucky few children will begin to consider proper spelling. When they say a word like *school*, they will hear distinct sounds. They will try to coordinate the sounds with letters and will end up with, maybe, *skl.* That's an improvement! Day by day, children of that sort will develop the ability to hear more sounds and to link the sounds to appropriate letters. They will memorize a certain number of spellings. In a delightfully short period of time they will write dozens and dozens of words correctly and automatically. They will concentrate on composing interesting stories and find it quite easy to record their thoughts on paper. Writing will be a breeze.

There are other children in first grade, however, for whom writing is not a breeze. Imagine such a child at the start of the school year. The teacher hands out sheets of blank paper and instructs the children to draw something that will help them remember their first week of first grade. She tells the children to add words to the page if they feel like doing so. Our first-grader draws a picture of his school building. Now he wants to write about his drawing. He wants to write the word *school*. He considers the first sound:

S-s-s-school. What letter makes that sound? He knows the answer—the letter *s*. But how do you form an *s*? Is this right?

How about this?

By the time the child gets an *s* on paper, he has forgotten the word he wanted to spell. So much effort and all he's got to show is a single letter! Considering the difficulty, it's not surprising that many children end up chewing pencils rather than writing with them.

A little instruction and practice may help this child; but then again, it may not. Many children continue to dread writing throughout their school years. Each passing day and each writing class or workshop makes these children more and more anxious. One child cannot think of a thing worth writing. Another has a zillion ideas but cannot focus on a single thought, and since you can only write one thought at a time, this child writes nothing at all. A third child gets so nervous he can't sit still long enough to write his name. A fourth writes only words he already knows how to spell. He writes the same story over and over: "I like to play." Then there is the child who only wants to write masterpieces. He starts lots of stories, but they all seem like failures and he refuses to finish any of them. These children all suffer from writer's block, except in a child's version, which is infinitely more painful and harmful than the adult version. At some time or another, virtually all children fall victim to such anxieties. Even the very best students suffer from these writer's worries on occasion.

What causes such discomfort with writing? In general, for first-, second-, and third-graders it's fairly easy to place the blame. The anxiety arises from the terrors of spelling and handwriting and the "but I have nothing to write" syndrome.

How to help your child overcome these difficulties? First, tackle the spelling question. Assure your child that when he is getting his ideas down on paper, correct spelling doesn't matter. Even with such encouragement, there are some children who will outright refuse to write unless they get help with spelling. When a child demands that I supply the correct letters, I comply. Sometimes I will dictate the letters. Other times I'll write words on a sheet of paper for the child to copy.

Second, tell your child not to worry about his handwriting. Tell him to ignore sloppy letters and reversed *d*'s. I usually promise to help children form correct letters after they have finished writing—if they want to do that. Occasionally a child completely forgets how to make an *f* or *w*. When that happens, I show him or her how to form the letters. Children get upset by such lapses in memory and often will refuse to keep writing unless they get immediate help.

It's a little harder to take on the "but I have nothing to write" problem. When children say this, they don't really mean they have nothing to write. They mean that they can't think of anything they feel comfortable writing. They are frightened by the idea of producing a whole story from beginning to end. They need less daunting writing projects. They need, in short, "Stress Busters."

A "Stress Buster" is a writing game or activity that is quick to complete and demands only a wee bit of writing from the participants. I try to make "Stress Busters" as silly and playful as possible. I ask children to make up menus for a restaurant that caters exclusively to monsters. I challenge them to engage in races with words, contests with words, and even a physical exercise with words. These games are popular with all children—those who write without hesitation as well as those who shy away from pencil and paper.

Of course, children still need encouragement to get through these activities. But encouragement is easy to give. Praise your child's efforts. Shrug off his errors. If you believe he is trying hard and treat him with the respect such effort deserves, your child will respond by producing the best work he possibly can.

"Stress Busters" are geared for first-, second-, and third-graders. Browse through this section, find a game that looks like it will be fun, and give it a try. If the game works—if it gets your child writing and smiling simultaneously—then you made a good choice. If not, try another game.

*C*hildren and adults talk and listen at rates of about 250 words per minute. No one can write so rapidly. Adults may get twenty-five words per minute onto paper. Children are slower.

GRADES

first and second

Even you, an experienced adult, cannot write unless you slow down your thinking. How does this work? When you write, you have a whole sentence in mind. You keep it in mind while you record words on paper—one word at a time. This can prove frustrating. You think of a wonderful sentence, start writing, get bogged down somewhere in the middle due to the necessity of spelling some horribly difficult word like *encyclopedia*, and by the time you have found your way back to the sentence, which was supposed to have a glorious ending, you are hopelessly lost.

This happens to all writers regardless of age, but children get bogged down more often than adults. Young writers launch themselves bravely into a sentence. They write the first couple of words. They push onward to word number three. But already they are faltering. By word number four, they have forgotten the sentence entirely. They are lost. They find it nearly impossible to think of a sentence and write it down in a single, stretched-out, slow-motion thought. With help, children can increase their ability to think in this specialized manner. That is the purpose of HALTING STORIES.

To start the game, ask your child to tell you a story—any story. He can recite Cinderella's saga, describe his day at school, or invent a tale on the spot. Children usually like to do that. But there is a hitch. Your child begins to talk, but before he has said more than a few words, you call out, "STOP!"

The child stops immediately. He doesn't say a word—until you shout, "GO!" Then he returns to the story. He must begin *exactly* where he left off. He continues the narrative, but before long you shout, "STOP!" again—and, soon enough, "GO!" That is the method of HALTING STORIES. You shouldn't wait long between each stop and go. A few seconds will do. Your child wins the game if he can finish his story without losing his place in spite of your interruptions.

You can play this game whenever you have five minutes to spare. Play as you walk to the park or while waiting on a supermarket line. If your fellow shoppers look perplexed as you shout, "STOP" and then, "GO," you can explain that today some serious learning is going on alongside the cauliflower and broccoli.

If your child wants you to take a turn telling a halting tale, go ahead and try. You will see ("STOP! . . . GO!") how hard it is to ("STOP! . . . GO!") stop and start your ("STOP! . . . GO!") stories.

Sara's sentence writing ability lasted for two words, maybe three. Then she got distracted. She would look up from her paper and offer to tell me how her weekend had gone. She was suddenly curious about the history of computers. Anything at all would have interested Sara if it could plausibly interrupt the grim task of writing a complete sentence.

Sara's problem was nervousness, not to say panic. How to get around this nervousness of hers? There was no point in chastising her. That would only make things worse. Pleading with her was also of no use. I had to find a way to help her relax—and still write. To distract her from her own nervousness while getting her to do the very thing that was making her nervous.

This is what I did. The next time she came to see me, I refused to greet her with words. Instead, I handed her this note.

> We are going to play a silent game today. No talking allowed.

Sara was puzzled. I explained—out loud—that for the next fifteen minutes neither of us could talk. Instead, we would commence a written conversation. No talking permitted. Well, *some* talking would be tolerable. If I wrote a word that Sara couldn't read, she could point to it and I would read it for her. Likewise, if she wrote a word I couldn't read, I would point and she could say it aloud. Any other talking was strictly forbidden.

If Sara blurted out words, I would rack up one point for each blurted word. If I talked, then Sara would get points. In case of a tie, Sara would be the winner.

"You mean all I have to do is not talk for fifteen minutes and I win?" Sara asked.

"That's all. Of course, we will be conversing the entire time. We will be writing our conversation, though. I'll write to you and you'll answer me. You can ask me any questions you want. You can change the subject of the conversation, but you must keep writing. I'll keep track of the time. Do you get the idea?" I asked.

SILENCE IS GOLDEN

GRADES

first, second, and third

MATERIALS

paper
pencil

"Got it," she answered.

"In that case, let the game begin."

Sara nodded her consent. I took out a piece of paper and wrote a question for her to answer.

What's the best thing about summer?

Sara took her pencil and responded:

It's fun. I don't hav srool.

I couldn't help smiling. Sara had written six words without so much as an interrupting peep. A major achievement! The game went on. Mostly I asked questions and Sara answered.

What's the best thing about winter?

I like snow

What do you do in the snow?

Sleding and I throe snowballs.

A few times, Sara looked ready to utter some crucial thought, but on each occasion she managed to control herself. In doing so, she won the game. This made her very happy. When I pointed out how many words she had written in just fifteen minutes, she was both happy and proud.

"Can we play this game again sometime?" she asked.

I wrote a note and handed it to her.

You can count on it.

What do monsters like to eat? Worms smothered in butterscotch sauce? Broiled mosquitoes with lizard livers? Old rags dipped in mud? Where can a hungry ogre or zombie get such delicacies? McDonald's? Wendy's? Of course not. Monsters must patronize special restaurants—MONSTER CAFES.

Matt, a second-grader who appreciated a good monster story, had no trouble imagining a restaurant catering exclusively to creepy creatures. He understood instantly the fun and challenge to be had in designing a menu for such an establishment. And although Matt hated most writing assignments, he was unreservedly enthusiastic about writing a menu for a MONSTER CAFE.

To begin our work, we took a sheet of paper and Matt drew a MONSTER CAFE logo on top.

We decided the cafe should offer two appetizers, two main courses, two desserts, and two beverages. I wrote appropriate section heads on the menu.

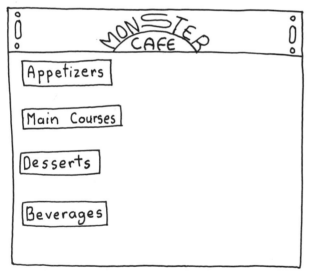

"Now for the hard part," I said. "We have to think of the right foods. Let's start with an appetizer."

It only took Matt a few moments to make an appalling suggestion: slimy guts with chocolate cockroaches. No discriminating

GRADES

first, second, and third

MATERIALS

paper
pencil
optional: crayons or colored markers

fiend could resist such delights. I suggested we charge $13.18 for this specialty of the house. Matt felt $313.18 was more appropriate. Ours was an establishment for wealthy monsters, he declared. Then he proudly wrote the first entry:

He asked for help spelling *cockroaches.* I obliged. He tackled *chocolate* on his own, with interesting results. Matt's unique spelling didn't disturb me. On the contrary, I was pleased that he attempted such a difficult word.

Next Matt suggested a thoroughly vile beverage: poison ivy sap. A monster could purchase this thirst-quencher for a mere $346.25. Item by item, we filled in the menu. We didn't finish in one sitting. Instead, we spent a few minutes of several tutoring sessions planning our cuisine. I wrote some entries, but in general Matt did the honors. After listing all the food, Matt decorated the menu with ghoulish designs.

The day we finished, Matt ran to the door as soon as his father arrived to pick him up and take him home from our tutoring session. As his dad walked through the door, Matt shoved the completed menu into his hands.

"Read this!" he demanded.

Matt's father and I had talked about spelling, so I knew he wouldn't be disturbed to see *cklt* instead of *chocolate* or *blud* in place of *blood.* He asked for a translation or two, then gave Matt the perfect response, "This is totally disgusting!"

Later that night, Matt's mother called with good news. Matt, who had never volunteered to write so much as his initials before, had spent an hour jotting grotesque goodies for Monster Cafe II.

Does your own child delight in the revolting? Then try composing a monster menu. Of course, your child might not be attracted to the repulsive. Your child might prefer making menus for an ice cream parlor that caters to circus clowns, a diner open exclusively to children, a fast-food joint frequented by aliens from outer space, or a Royal Cafe that serves only kings, queens, princes, and princesses. Royal food must be pure and refined; that menu won't include a single pickled worm. Tastes vary. The repulsive path is best for some children, but not for all.

A RACE OF WORDS

Hannah couldn't wait to start first grade. She desperately wanted to read and write. She was positive that after a week or two, she would be reading fluently and writing prolifically. It didn't happen. Weeks and weeks went by, and a frustrated Hannah made no headway whatsoever.

By February, her slow progress worried her parents and teacher. Hannah herself was miserable. Every night she told her mom how stupid she felt. Her mother protested, but Hannah could prove she was stupid. All her friends were reading and writing. Her best friend, Alice, had finished writing a story and it was *six* pages long. Clearly, if Alice was smart (and everyone agreed she was), then Hannah was an idiot (no matter what her loving parents said).

In March, Hannah gave up. She didn't want to try anymore. It was too painful. When her teacher assigned written work, Hannah handed in a crumpled, smeared sheet on which she had written one or two words. A month later, her parents sent Hannah to me for tutoring.

By that time, Hannah had taught herself dozens of clever ways to *avoid* putting pencil to paper. My first task, therefore, was to reignite her excitement and enthusiasm for writing. Competition, I've found, can make for effective kindling. Reluctant writers will often scrawl a few words, if doing so means they win a game. The particular game I chose for Hannah was A RACE OF WORDS.

To begin, I told her to look around my workroom. The room was filled with furniture, books, odds and ends. For the next ten minutes, Hannah's job was to write the names of everything she could see in the room. She had to write fast, because she wanted to list as many objects as possible. She wrote for five minutes, while I sat quietly. After five minutes, though, I began a list of my own. We both wrote for the next five minutes. When time was up, we scored our lists. I got one point for every item I recorded. Hannah got one point for every item on her list that was also on mine. But she got *three* points for anything she noted that I had failed to include. I did not get this three-point advantage.

Spelling didn't matter. Speed and thoroughness were everything. From the first, Hannah approved of this contest. True, she had to write, but only one word at a time. Best of all, with her time and point advantage, Hannah felt she had a chance to win. Secretly I was rooting for Hannah. If she won the first game, she would probably want to play again and again. So I wrote slowly and paused between words.

When time ran out, I had ten words on my list for a total of ten points.

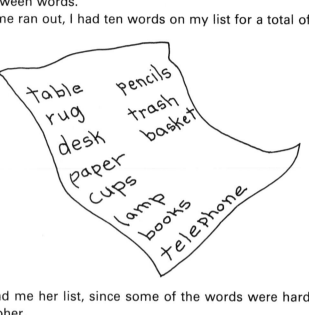

Hannah read me her list, since some of the words were hard for me to decipher.

Even Hannah was baffled by *dzc*. "Could it be *desk*?" I guessed. That was it. Hannah had written just seven words, but she had three words that did not appear on my own list and which therefore counted for three points each. These words were *rsr* (eraser), *flr* (floor), and *rshr* (rocking chair). All in all, she accumulated thirteen points.

What if Hannah couldn't remember the meaning of *dzc* and I couldn't figure it out for her? We would have crossed the word off her list and then given her thirty seconds to add a new word.

Just as I hoped, Hannah's enthusiasm for A RACE OF WORDS increased after her victory. During the following weeks we raced often. We listed animals, TV shows, colors, desserts, sports, girls' names, boys' names, fruits, things that use electricity, and things that most everyone hates. Sometimes I rigged our races in Hannah's favor, but not always.

In a few weeks, Hannah's attitude toward writing changed—a little. She didn't dread pencils. She didn't cringe at the sight of paper. Instead, she was eager to write, at least at game time. The game gave Hannah confidence. And soon enough there was a spillover: Hannah agreed to try more substantial writing tasks. We still had a long way to go, but A RACE OF WORDS gave Hannah a fresh start.

If I were allowed to use only a single activity to help a reluctant child overcome qualms about writing, I would pick WORD BY WORD. Children like this game, whether or not they like to write.

The first step in WORD BY WORD is to choose a title for the story you are about to write. The title should indicate something about the upcoming plot. Here are some sample titles, but you can certainly make up your own.

Hunting for Dinosaurs
Halloween in a Haunted House
The Day I Scared a Monster
Lost in the Woods
The Magic Spell
The Mad Scientist Strikes Again

Once you select a title, you and your child start writing the story—together. You write a little and then your child adds a bit. Exactly how many words will you each contribute? To determine that you must roll a playing die. Let's say you throw a four. That means you write the first four words of the story. Not three words, not five, but exactly four, as required by the roll of the die.

This morning I went

Now, hand the die to your child and let him roll. Let's say he gets a one. That means he supplies one, and only one, word to the story.

This morning I went for

WORD BY WORD

MATERIALS

paper
pencil
one playing die

Your turn again: roll and write. Add a few words, and then pass the die to your child.

This morning I went for a

walk in The park.

Keep rolling and writing until the story ends.

Sometime during the game your child may moan, "I threw a two, but I have more to say." When that happens, be sympathetic but firm. Don't allow him to write more words than the die dictates. This is the Tom Sawyer method of pedagogy. Remember Tom painting his fence? Tom bragged about the delights of painting while refusing to let his friends help with the job. As a result, his friends insisted on painting and cheerfully completed all of his hard work. According to this principle, you should forbid any extra words while playing WORD BY WORD. You'll see—soon writing may be irresistibly appealing.

What happens if your child runs out of ideas? Talk together about the plot. Make suggestions and ponder possibilities. This is a collaborative effort, after all.

At some point—often before the story reaches a natural conclusion—a child will run out of energy for writing. When I see a youngster getting fatigued, I suggest that we each take just three more turns. Even tired writers are willing to do that much. This does pose a creative challenge, however. You must invent an ending within your word limits. Sometimes at the end of a story, I bend the rules and let the child dictate a few sentences to finish our saga. There are times, though, when a story is too good to end abruptly. In that case, tuck it away in a safe place. In a day, or a week, pull it out again, grab pencils, roll the die, and go on with the tale.

MAKE A LIST

Imagine you must fight a gigantic fire-breathing dragon. You can take ten weapons with you. What will you select? A fire extinguisher? A laser gun? A net made of flame-resistant rope?

GRADES

first and second

MATERIALS

paper
pencil

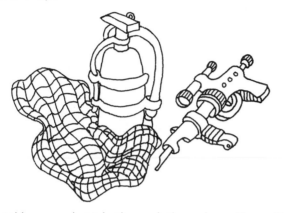

Imagine taking a rocket trip through the galaxy. You will be alone in space for an entire year. After the essential equipment is loaded on the ship, what extra ten items will you pack? A book? A lap-top computer? A space camera? A gigantic box of cream-filled chocolates?

You have just met a witch. You ask her to teach you how to cast a magic spell. What five things will you do for her in exchange? Clean her cave for a month? Bake her gingerbread cookies? Care for her cat? Re-twig her broom?

Writing lists like these was Noah's favorite way to start a tutoring session. Lists were, for a time, the only writing he could bear.

Noah, a second-grader, was supposed to write in school, of course. His teacher set aside forty-five minutes a day for writing. During this time, the kids in Noah's class all worked on stories. Some wrote true stories. Some wrote imaginary adventures. In general, everyone had something to write—except Noah. By January, all the other kids in his class had written between three and four lengthy tales. Noah had lots of first lines for lots of stories. But after an opening paragraph, he gave up. As a result, he hadn't come close to finishing even one story.

This was very odd, and Noah's teacher knew it. Noah was one of the best and most enthusiastic readers in her class. Such readers are, as a rule, good or at least willing writers. It seems, however, that Noah didn't care about this rule. His problem was a lack of confidence. He didn't feel he could produce stories that he would feel proud of having written. The standards he set for himself were impossibly high. He wanted to write stories as polished as those of his favorite authors—E. B. White and A. A. Milne. Every time he started a story, he gave up.

To break this pattern, Noah needed some unqualified successes as a writer. Clearly, if I asked him to write something as intimidating as a story, he would balk, just as he did in his regular classroom. But writing lists was a different matter.

The first list had to be special. It had to trigger Noah's imagination. What list did I pick? "Five Ways to Make a Teacher Mad." If the child feels relaxed enough, I know—from numerous experiences—that this list can get wonderfully wacky. I suspected, though, that Noah would need encouragement before he could feel free to share any sensationally shocking ideas. With this in mind, I offered him a few suggestions intended to startle him.

"I can think of some strange ways to make a teacher mad," I said. "You could dump live frogs in her soup at lunch or spray her hair with skunk stink juice. That would make *me* mad. I wonder if you can think of anything along those lines?"

Noah was astonished. Such ideas coming from an adult! When he got over his amazement, he assured me that he could match my level of skullduggery. His ideas were impressive.

put gum in her hair
trip her
put mushy rotten tomato on her chair
put mud in her coffee
put a snake in her hat

It took Noah about fifteen minutes to finish his list. In those minutes, he had written more words than he had composed in months of school. Why did Noah write so much on this one day? The list structure was easy for him to control. He only had to think of one idea at a time. There were no characters, no plot, no events to organize. A list is a modest thing to write. It eliminates the psychological weight of creating a story. Also, the assignment appealed to him. It gave him a safe way to express some of his pent-up frustration about school and teachers.

Noah had done an excellent job, and I told him so. "You made me laugh," I said. "It takes writing talent to make a reader laugh. I also like how you describe things. You didn't just say a tomato, you called it a mushy, rotten tomato. Those two words made it unpleasantly real. That's what good writing is about. I'm impressed."

Noah didn't say anything, but his smile proved that my words mattered. Writers—young and old—thrive on compliments.

Week by week, list by list, Noah's confidence grew. Maybe he was a capable writer, after all. Maybe he could attempt writing a story. He decided to try—in school. What a transformation! Now during writing time, Noah produced story after story after story.

Perhaps your child will find MAKE A LIST appealing. If you think so, scan the following list of lists. Select a promising one and start writing. It's probably best if you write the first few items. As your child catches on, he can take over. Of course, you could take turns until the list is full. You could both write five items separately and secretly before sharing your ideas. There are dozens of variations when it comes to writing lists. Try different methods until you find the perfect system for you and your child.

A List of Lists

    5 totally new flavors of ice cream
    6 gifts you would give a friendly giant
    5 ways to stop a ghost from moving into your house
    5 places you would go if you could be invisible for three hours
    3 wishes you would make if you found a wishing well (You
       can't wish for more wishes, though.)
    6 things you can do with a book—aside from reading it
    7 ways to make a friend jealous
    5 reasons why your birthday should be celebrated three times
       a year

Persuading Sam to write was exhausting work. He even resisted signing his name. He didn't like reading, either. After a month of working with Sam, I had yet to stumble on a single book he found acceptable. So, with Sam in mind, I went book shopping. On a hunch, I purchased a collection of tongue twisters. The next time Sam came for tutoring, I presented him with the volume. He grabbed it—a good omen. He opened the book—even better. He agreed to read a twister: *Six thick thistle sticks.* We took turns trying to get our tongues around it, but had no success. Yet Sam wasn't complaining about reading. That was success enough.

Sam agreed to read some more. Occasionally, he interrupted his reading to share a twister that wasn't in the book.

Now if Sam was willing—almost eager—to read tongue twisters, mightn't he be willing—even eager—to write one or two? I closed the book and announced that it was time for writing. Sam grimaced and started to object. I quickly added that today he could write a tongue twister if he wanted. He could copy one from the book we were reading or he could write an old favorite.

"I can do that," he said with relief. I gave him a sheet of paper and he started writing.

she sells seshls by the seshr

Sure, there were mistakes. But he and I could both read the twister—although neither of us could say it three times quickly. And then, amazingly, Sam asked to write a second tongue twister.

Why did tongue twisters have this effect? There were two reasons. First, the words were already set. Sam didn't have to imagine anything. All he had to do was say the twister slowly and write one word at a time. Second, Sam, like most children, loved tongue twisters. He thought it was neat, therefore, to record a few favorites.

Since Sam had gotten so excited about this work, I suggested that over the next several weeks we write a collection of tongue twisters. When we had a good amount, we could bind them to-

GRADES

first, second, and third

MATERIALS

paper
pencil
stapler
construction paper
optional: a joke book

gether into a book. If he wanted, I added, he could include jokes and riddles in his collection. It would be an assortment of sillies— A SILLY BOOK. Sam thought this was a great idea. He wanted to write the second page right away, and he wanted to write a riddle. He took a sheet of paper and got to work. After he finished writing, we shared the job of illustrating the first two pages of his SILLY BOOK.

Session after session, going one joke, riddle, or tongue twister at a time, we eventually compiled a weighty manuscript: twelve pages. We made a construction-paper cover and stapled all the sheets together. Sam was proud of himself. He never thought he could write so much. He had certainly never thought he could ever write a book! He was willing now—at least sometimes, and with a gentle prod—to write a handful of words without complaining. That was progress.

Your child might like to make A SILLY BOOK at home with you. You might have trouble coming up with the right material, though. If that happens, poke around in a children's joke book or tongue-twister book. You'll find some titles in the Appendix: Books for Reading Aloud.

LET'S ARGUE

Which is sweeter—a dish of vanilla ice cream or a kiss?

Which number is more important—two or six?

Who is more powerful—Dracula or Superman?

Who is a better debater—you or your child?

If you really want to find out, play LET'S ARGUE. Roger and I played with delightful results. How did the debate start? Roger, who was very fond of his golden retriever, declared that dogs make better pets than cats. As a serious cat person, I could not let his declaration go unchallenged. So I proposed a debate.

For the debate, Roger would write five reasons why dogs make better pets. I would write five reasons why cats are preferable. Then we would compare arguments. Perhaps there would be a clear winner. If not, we would wait for Roger's mother to come pick him up at the end of his tutoring session. Then I would read both papers to her. Naturally, I would not disclose the author of either paper. After listening, she would decide which list was more convincing.

Roger loved the whole idea, but he was unsure how to begin. I offered to write my list first and show it to him. Perhaps my arguments would offer inspiration.

GRADES

second and third

MATERIALS

paper
pencil
a judge

---

① Cats are soft and warm.

② It feels so nice when a cat purrs.

③ You don't have to walk a cat in the ice and snow.

④ Cats will catch mice and sometimes cockroaches.

⑤ You never have to give a cat a bath.

Let's Argue

Roger was impressed. He thought the cockroach bit especially effective. And thus inspired, he was eager to compose his own arguments.

① Dogs re frde — Dogs are friendly.

② Dogs go swig — Dogs go swimming.

③ Dogs eet fud ew dn lick — Dogs eat food you don't like.

④ Dogs pla cach in the prk — Dogs play catch in the park.

⑤ Dogs rnt scrdf cats — Dogs aren't scardy cats.

Roger's spelling was atrocious. That's why I have provided translation into standard spelling. His handwriting was horrifying. I didn't care. In all of Roger's seven years, he had never written so much in a single sitting. As I clapped my hands in appreciation, my office doorbell rang. Roger's mom—our official judge—walked in. Roger jumped up shouting, "Mom, you have to decide who's best, me or Peggy."

Roger's mom looked confused. I explained the situation, and then I read the papers. Roger's mother barely kept her composure. She figured out which paper was Roger's, of course. She instantly understood that this amount of writing and this level of enthusiasm for writing was very special. She calmly declared the dog argument superior. Roger leapt up, shouting, "Yes, yes, yes! That's me! I won!" Roger's mother acted suitably surprised while offering her congratulations.

The next time we worked together, Roger wanted—indeed insisted on—another debate. We picked a new topic. (I argued that popcorn tops all snacks. Roger fought for potato chips.) This time Roger and I worked on our lists simultaneously. He needed no help in developing his ideas.

To play at home, you will need debating topics and a judge. The judge has an important job, but it's not a time-consuming one. The judge doesn't even have to be in the house. You can telephone—or even fax—an aunt, grandmother, or family friend and get a long-distance referee. If no judge is available, you can hold on to your debate pages until someone is free to arbitrate. Or you can dispense with the judge altogether and evaluate the debates on your own.

As for topics, here's a list of argumentative ideas you can use.

Yes or no, children should pick their own bedtimes.
Yes or no, children should be allowed to eat whatever they want.
Which is better, living in the city or living in the country?
Which is better, Halloween or Thanksgiving?
Which would be better, the power to read people's minds or having one million dollars in cash?
Who is worse, a very wicked witch or Dracula?
Which is the better sport, baseball or football?

If LET'S ARGUE is a hit in your house, play as often as you want. Why argue with success?

DO IT

GRADES

first, second, and third

MATERIALS

paper
pencil

Warning: don't play this game if you're tired or lacking in physical energy. In my experience, DO IT is universally appealing to children. It is less than universally appealing to adults, however, especially on lazy days. In this game, you write a physical challenge for your child on a slip of paper. You might direct him to jump in the air five times, or tiptoe to the window, or do three sit-ups, or spin around six times. Your child reads the instruction and attempts the assignment.

Then, however, you are obliged to switch roles. Your child writes a physical challenge for you. He might order you to crawl to the desk, hop to the kitchen, or touch your toes sixteen times. And you will have to do as commanded.

You can set limits. I once outright refused even to attempt a hundred push-ups. But too many restrictions take the fun out of the game. The fun, for your child, is commanding you to embark on a series of daunting physical exertions. The more you moan and groan, the more your child will giggle with pleasure. If you fail altogether, well, nothing could be better—from your child's point of view. For you, the fun is watching your child enthusiastically write instruction after instruction. To my complete delight, I've known children to insist on writing more, more, and more, so long as it forces me to work out harder, harder, and harder. Adults know that learning to write is like learning to play catch or the piano: you must practice. Wise adults know that if the practice is fun or silly, children aren't likely to complain.

Spelling is not important in this game, nor is grammar. It doesn't matter if a child leaves out an occasional word. You will almost always be able to figure out what is expected of you, and if you cannot, just ask. Your child will happily explain.

*I*f you could plan a perfect day, selecting all your favorite activities with no restrictions, what would you do? See a movie? Read a book? Go swimming? Eat buttered snails in a four-star French restaurant?

If fantasizing about a perfect day appeals to you, you will enjoy SCHEDULES. Your model day will start at 9:00 A.M. and last until 8:00 P.M. Your job is to record each event, hour by hour. There is only one rule: you must include a minimum of eight different activities. In other words, you cannot spend the entire day lounging on the beach. You must rouse yourself for water skiing or a lobster lunch.

Meanwhile your child should construct a wonderful day of his own. What is his idea of perfection? You will find out by taking two sheets of paper and fixing each one up to look like a date book, one for yourself and one for the child. Then start writing.

Here are two sample pages. I wrote one. A third-grader named Julie created the other.

GRADES

second and third

MATERIALS

paper
pencil

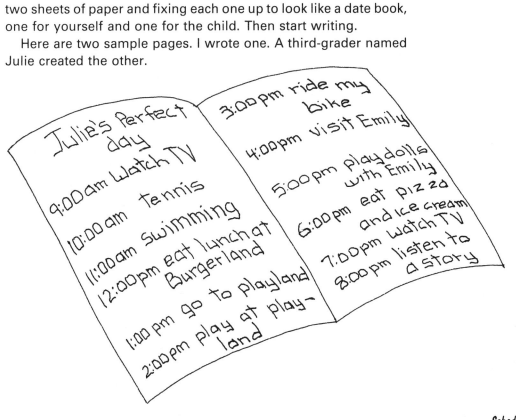

Julie's Perfect day
9:00am Watch TV
10:00am tennis
11:00am Swimming
12:00pm eat lunch at Burgerland
1:00pm go to playland
2:00pm play at playland
3:00pm ride my bike
4:00pm visit Emily
5:00pm play dolls with Emily
6:00pm eat pizza and ice cream
7:00pm watch TV
8:00pm listen to a story

Peggy's Perfect day

9:00 am Breakfast in bed
10:00 am Read a book
11:00 am Go to the beach
12:00 pm Picnic lunch at the beach
1:00 pm swimming in the ocean
2:00 pm Jog on the beach

3:00 pm Helicopter ride to the city
4:00 pm Visit a friend
5:00 pm Go to an art museum
6:00 pm stay in the museum
7:00 pm Dinner at a Japanese restaurant
8:00 pm Read a book while eating pie

Julie liked this activity, and she worked hard writing her ideas. But when she suggested designing a second perfect day, I rejected the idea.

Perfection should be unique—a one-time thing. We did, however, come up with some other schedules. We plotted the worst conceivable day. Then we made schedules for other people, real and imagined. We created a schedule for Cinderella, Humpty-Dumpty, the Wicked Witch of the West, Julie's two-year-old cousin, and Santa Claus. Sometimes we worked together on the same schedule, but usually we worked independently.

Try SCHEDULES at your house. If you like the game, you might end up scheduling it into your week on a regular basis.

Schedule for the Wicked Witch

9:00 am Make brew
10:00 am Visit ghosts
11:00 am Chop rat's liver

*T*ake a look at this list:

1. I had a hamburger for lunch.
2. I called someone in California today.
3. I love washing dishes.
4. My new shoes hurt my toes.
5. I read the newspaper this morning.

GRADES

second and third

MATERIALS

paper
pencil

I wrote it. It contains three true statements and two lies. If we were playing IS IT TRUE? I would hand you my list and you would try to determine which sentences are true. You would put a *T* (for *True*) next to each of those. You would put an *L* (for *Lies*) next to the two potential falsehoods. Each correct guess racks up five points. Did you mark 2, 4, and 5 with a *T*? Did you mark 1 and 3 with an *L*? Then you earned twenty-five points in this round of IS IT TRUE? All five statements *might* have been true, but two of them happened not to be.

If you play IS IT TRUE? at home, you and your child will each write a list. Then you will exchange papers. After you have both filled in *T*'s and *L*'s, you'll go over the lists and tally points. You need to accumulate fifty points to win this game, so even if you lose the first round, you still have a chance.

I have found IS IT TRUE? to be a very popular game. Why do children like it? I think they like ferreting out my secrets. And they enjoy fooling me with their lies. I'm partial to IS IT TRUE? because it gets children writing without inhibitions. Isn't that worth stretching the truth a bit?

BRAGGING CONTESTS

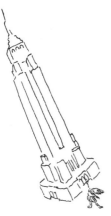

Sascha liked to brag. According to him, he ate six pepperoni pizza pies for dinner. He slammed a baseball so hard, he split the ball in two. Last month, he taught his dog a thousand tricks. And he didn't go to sleep at all over the weekend. Instead, he stayed up all night Saturday and all night Sunday playing Nintendo. Sascha was a weaver of tall tales. He and Paul Bunyan had a lot in common.

Given Sascha's fondness for exaggeration, I thought he would enjoy a BRAGGING CONTEST. The rules are simple. Contestants take turns bragging about one subject—for instance, the brute strength of each player. With every turn, you write a statement that's more astonishing than your opponent's last claim. If you can outdo your opponent, the game goes on. When one player's mind goes blank, the game ends.

Here's what I wrote to begin a contest with Sascha:

I'm so strong, I can lift the Empire State Building with one hand.

Could Sascha top that? He did by writing:

I can lift a mountain with my pinky

Now I had to devise something even more outlandish:

I am stronger than you. I can pick up an erupting volcano and toss it in the ocean.

Sascha countered with:

I can lift the ocean

"Wow, you got me, Sascha," I said after reading this wild invention. "I can't think of a bigger brag. You're the winner."

To be honest, I *could* have dreamed up a more extravagant boast—picking up the galaxy, for instance. I chose not to for two reasons. First, I didn't want to tax Sascha with another round of the game. Two brags was, for Sascha, a lot of writing. Second, you only get a winner in this game when one player concedes defeat. Imagine Sascha announcing, "Peggy, your brag was so good, I can't think of a better one." Never; it would never happen. Unless I conceded, the game would have gone on till midnight. I didn't mind losing. Sascha had done a great job. He deserved victory.

You can make your own BRAGGING CONTESTS last longer—assuming that you and your child are both enjoying yourselves. You don't have to brag about physical prowess. You can boast about other talents and abilities. Here's a list to get you going:

> I'm so strong, I . . .
> I'm so rich, I . . .
> I'm so sneaky, I . . .
> I'm so smart, I . . .
> I'm so silly, I . . .
> I'm so tall, I . . .
> I'm so magical, I . . .
> I'm so fast, I . . .

When you play, something extraordinary may happen. Your child may discover how much he likes writing. And that's not a brag. That's a real possibility.

RHYME TIME

For some children, poetry offers the best and fastest way to dispel the terrors of writing. Poetry's first advantage is its brevity. Four or five lines can make a very fine poem, which is reassuring to any young child who trembles at the thought of having to write at great length. Poetry's second advantage is its lightness. A silly poem can be a good poem. That, too, is reassuring. And there is a third advantage. Many children seem to gravitate naturally toward poetry. They enjoy listening to poetry read aloud. Sometimes they memorize poems just by hearing them.

Kate, a second-grader, was like that. She hated writing, but she loved poetry. She could even recite a few favorite verses that had been read aloud to her. With that in mind, I suggested, as a way to get her writing, that we compose a poem together. At first she balked.

"I can't write rhymes," she said hoping to quash any new demands on her.

I reminded her that poems don't have to rhyme. Kate was skeptical. She viewed rhymeless poetry as inherently inferior.

"In that case, I have a way to help you make a rhyming poem," I said. "Want to try it?"

I put a couple of sheets of paper and two pencils on the table.

"First, we need two lists of rhyming words. Let's start with *boat.* How many different words can you think of that rhyme with boat?"

"There's *coat* and *goat.* That's all, I think."

I wrote these words on a sheet of paper. "Those are good words. There are more, though, and I know how to find them."

I jotted letters on a sheet of paper. The sheet looked like this:

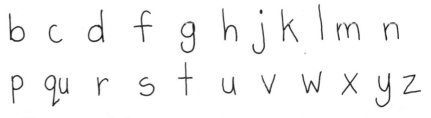

These were all the consonants in the alphabet. Then I jotted down a large number of what are called "blended consonants" (*bl,*

cl, *st*, etc.) and "digraphs" (*sh*, *ch*, etc.). This new list looked like this:

bl br ch cl cr dr fl fr
gl gr pl pr sc scr sh shr
sr st sw th thr tr wh wr

The purpose of putting all these consonants on the page was to help me find rhyming words. Skimming the letters with *boat* still in mind, I stumbled on the letters *fl*. *Boat* led to *float*, an excellent new rhyme. Also, I hoped that Kate would, in time, study the list along with me.

I said to her, "I'm looking for a letter that will help us make a rhyme. There's *n*." I pointed to it. "With an *n*, we can change *boat* into *note*."

"Note—boat," Kate said. "Yeah, that rhymes."

"I'll write it down on a new sheet of paper. *Note* and *boat* aren't spelled alike, the way *boat* and *goat* are, but they certainly do rhyme. Now, how about a word that begins with *thr*?"

"Throat!" Kate shouted.

Throat went on our list. After a few minutes we had collected nine words on our new sheet.

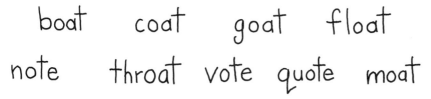

boat   coat   goat   float

note   throat vote quote moat

There are other possibilities, of course, but nine words would do for our purposes. Besides, we had to conserve our rhyming energy to create a second list. The kind of poem I had in mind requires at least two different rhymes. I proposed a new word, *stop*. Now we looked for words to rhyme with *stop*. We found quite a few.

stop   hop   pop top
slop   chop   drop flop mop

It took about ten minutes to develop our word collections. Once we had completed this job, we started the poem. Kate had the task of composing the first line. This line had to end with a word from the *boat*/*coat* list. Kate took a minute to study the list. Then she dictated a line, which I inscribed on a fresh sheet of paper:

I have a big goat.

"Nice," I said after I finished writing. "You'll be happy to know that it's up to me to create the next line. I want it to rhyme with your contribution. So I will end with a *boat*/*coat* word, too. But not *goat*, since you already used it."

I puzzled over the list before writing:

I have a big goat.
He wears a wool coat.

"That's two lines," I said. "Now we need a third, and you're going to write it. This line should end with a word from the *stop*/*hop* group. Can you write a line like that?"

Kate composed a humorous bit that she, all by herself, wrote down on the paper.

I have a big goat.
He wears a wool coat.
He eats lots of slop,

If Kate had run into trouble composing this or any other line, I would have smoothed her way. How? By suggesting poetic possibilities. As it was, I needed to muster my own literary powers to produce the fourth line. It had to rhyme with line number three.

I have a big goat.
He wears a wool coat.
He eats lots of slop,
And cleans up with a mop.

That was pretty good. In a fit of ambition, I suggested that, having achieved such dazzling results with four lines, we trudge onward with a fifth or sixth line. The best thing was to return to the *boat/goat* list and look for another rhyme. Kate and I pored over the list. We pondered, we experimented, and, at last, in a burst of inspiration, we composed the final couplet. Our poem was finished. It went like this:

I have a big goat.
He wears a wool coat.
He eats lots of slop,
And cleans up with a mop.
He sails on a boat
With a noodle in his throat.

The part about the noodle was extremely puzzling, and gave our poem a somewhat curious ending. Oh, well, many is the time when I have read a poem that I could not fully understand.

The next time we worked together, Kate asked to write a new poem. She had never asked to write anything before, but now she wanted to return to poetry. So I knew that the goat with the noodle in his throat was, in fact, a great triumph. The new poem required two new sets of rhyming words. We also decided—it was I who made the decision, actually—to vary our rhyme pattern. The poem about the goat followed the pattern of AA-BB-AA. But this time we composed our poem according to the rhyme scheme A-B-A-B-A-B. It was up to me to propose the two rhymes. I suggested one list of words rhyming with *back* and a second list rhyming with *light*. Then I wrote out the consonants on a sheet of paper and we began looking for rhymes. We found *back*, *lack*, *sack*, *rack*, *snack*, and I wrote them down. *Light* was just as simple: *light*, *night*, *fight*, *white*, *right*.

It's true that poems composed by means of rhyme lists tend to end up silly and nonsensical. But that is their appeal. Laughter and learning are not contradictory. As one poet has written:

> You can do worse
> Than to toil at verse.
> Rhyming may weary us,
> But its purpose is serious:
> To make learning to write
> A child's delight.

Don Quixote de la Mancha was a slightly mad knight, but he had several good ideas, and one of his best was to commission a poem dedicated to his true love, Dulcinea del Toboso. He asked the poet to start each line of this verse with a letter of Dulcinea's name. This may be the first reference to a rare but lovely form of poetry called acrostics. In an acrostic, you can read the first letter of each line down the page and you will discover a word, a message, perhaps a person's name. It may be that you and your child will enjoy creating acrostic verses. You might begin with a tribute to summer.

Write the letters *S U M M E R* on a sheet of paper like this:

ACROSTIC POEMS

GRADES

first, second, and third

MATERIALS

paper
pencil
optional: oaktag or craft paper
and colored markers

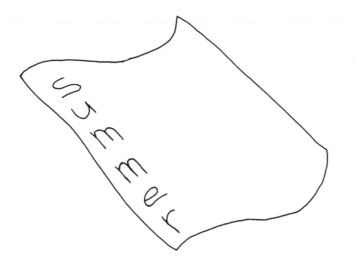

Now think of summer delights. Consider the many qualities that make summer special. Can you describe those wonderful summertime qualities with words or phrases that begin with the letter *s*? *Sunny*, *surf*, *scorcher*, *showers*, *swimming*, *solar*, *sultry*, and *sand* are good possibilities. Which of these words conjures the season most vividly? *Sunny* is an excellent choice. Write *sunny* on the top row. Since the letter *s* is already in place, you merely add the letters *unny*. Better yet, have your child write those letters.

S unny
u
m
m
e
r

That leaves *summer*'s next letter, which happens to be *u*. What could possibly be a summertime word or phrase that begins with *u*? A few ideas come to mind—for instance, *umbrellas on the beach*, or *underwater swimming*. You could always get desperate and use a word like *unwintery*, which is kind of cheating, except that with letters like *u* it's sometimes hard not to cheat. And having found a word or phrase for *u*, you must now move along to *m, m, e,* and finally *r*, in each case writing down your chosen words and phrases. Here's a version of summer:

S unny
Umbrellas on the beach
magical
moonlight swims
easy living
relaxation

Read the words out loud: "Sunny, umbrellas on the beach, magical, moonlight swims, easy living, relaxation." That's a summertime ACROSTIC POEM. Maybe it's not the greatest poem ever written. Still a poem is a poem, even if, as in this case, it has neither rhyme nor a steady rhythm.

I've used ACROSTIC POEMS with dozens of students. Somehow

they are always fun to write. When you create an ACROSTIC POEM you can begin with any word you want: your name, your child's name, your pet's nickname, a favorite storybook character, a sports team, a holiday.

ACROSTIC POEMS are useful, too. For instance, they make excellent birthday cards. Fold a sheet of paper so that it looks like a greeting card. On the front, write the appropriate name in the proper acrostic manner and fill in celebratory words. The more colorful and elegant the lettering the better. Inside the card, draw a picture or write a greeting.

The next time you're expecting a houseguest, try making a jumbo acrostic welcome sign. Buy a large sheet of oaktag or craft paper. Now write your guest's name in colored marker lettering down the left-hand side of the paper. Start composing the poem. When you're finished, surround your work with a garland of WEL-COME WELCOME WELCOME.

Shining Sonia
Our friend
Now she is here
In our house
Are we happy? YES!

If you and your child have trouble thinking of appropriate words, turn to a dictionary. Skimming through the listings for *m* in a children's dictionary, I discovered all these wonderful entries: *magical, magnetic, majestic, marvelous, masterpiece.* I found them without going past *ma.* Imagine what I might have found by moving ahead a few pages to *me* or *mi*! Sharing the dictionary with your child is a fine idea under any circumstances, but it's especially fine when the purpose is clear: Let's give Sonia a grand hello!

ONE QUESTION, PLEASE

Betsy was a bright second-grader who liked outsmarting adults. That is why she enjoyed playing ONE QUESTION, PLEASE. The game combines a guessing tournament and a writing contest. With a little luck, a clever child can outmaneuver an unwitting adult, which is always a thrill.

Before the action could begin, Betsy and I both had to think of a secret animal. Any animal would do—a wild beast, a pet, an insect, a fish, or a fowl. I settled on a rabbit. But I didn't write *rabbit* anywhere; I kept the word in my head. I had no idea what animal Betsy had picked, of course. The challenge for me was to identify her selection before she could zero in on my rabbit. If I could, victory would be mine.

We needed to be cautious, however. Players who guess incorrectly automatically lose the game. But, by means of written words, Betsy and I could question each other and in that manner slowly close in on the other's mystery animal. The search for information was limited, though. We could only ask questions whose answers were "yes," "no," "yes and no," "sometimes," "maybe," or "I don't know." And we could ask only one question at a time.

Once I was sure that Betsy understood the rules, I composed a question for her to answer,

Do people ever keep your animal as a pet?

And she wrote one for me.

Is your animal fery?

GRADE

third

MATERIALS

paper
pencil

When we finished, we switched papers. I didn't complain about "fery." ONE QUESTION, PLEASE is a writing game, not a spelling game. Anyway, I knew she meant "furry." I wrote my answer to her question:

Rabbits are covered with fur; that's for sure.

Meanwhile, she wrote an answer to my question:

Now Betsy knew that I'd selected a furry beast and I knew that her animal was not a pet. Neither of us knew enough to guess yet, so we each wrote another question. I asked:

Betsy asked:

And then we gave each other honest answers.

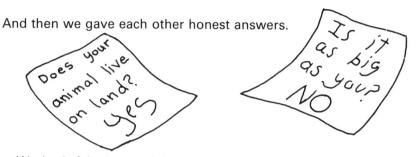

We both felt the need for more information, so we continued writing questions and answers. After several more rounds, I knew that Betsy had picked a vegetarian land animal that climbs trees, might or might not like bananas, and is not a household pet. I had a lot of information, but Betsy's animal still eluded me. Betsy knew that my animal was furry, smaller than me, eats vegetables, can be a pet, does not bark, and has a tail and pointy ears.

She put these facts together and announced, "I think I know your animal."

"Are you positive?" I asked. "Remember, you lose the game if you're wrong."

"I think it's a rabbit," she said, a little hesitantly.

"You got it!" I replied. "I wish I knew your animal, but I'm still confused. What is it?"

"A koala bear!" she shouted.

"I had no idea," I said truthfully.

Betsy wrote a considerable number of words during this game, but she didn't complain once. In fact, she asked when we could play again. That's why this game is a stress buster. It gets children like Betsy writing without complaining. And if a child writes enough questions and answers, he may notice that writing isn't so hard to do after all. And if writing isn't so hard, well then, maybe it's not such a bad way to spend time.

What if your child dislikes animals? You can play the game with a secret food, a city, a famous person, or a household object instead.

If the game is a success in your house, you may find yourself writing questions during long car rides or while waiting for the dentist. One question seems to lead to another.

One Question, Please

THAT'S GOOD/
THAT'S BAD

GRADES

second and third

MATERIALS

paper
pencil
oaktag or posterboard
paper fastener
scissors

I went to the zoo yesterday. That's good. I forgot to bring any money and couldn't get in. That's bad. I found a dollar bill on the sidewalk and used it for the admission fee. That's good. I wanted to see the monkeys, but the monkey house was closed. That's bad. The guard let me in anyway. That's good. The biggest monkey threw a banana at me. That's bad. I caught it in my right hand. That's good. The banana was mushy and it got all over my hand. That's bad.

Such is the beginning of a good/bad story. In a good/bad tale, luck is followed by misfortune and misfortune leads back to luck. You can find good/bad books in libraries and bookstores, but I suggest you and your child consider writing your own. How? By playing a competitive writing game called, appropriately enough, THAT'S GOOD/THAT'S BAD. Your child will never have to write more than two sentences at a time while playing. That's not stressful. And yet the two of you together will create a delightfully silly story.

To play this game you will need a spinner. It's easy to make one. Begin by cutting a piece of oaktag or cardboard into a circle. Divide the circle into four sections, and label the sections as in this illustration.

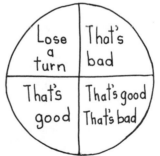

Cut an arrow out of oaktag, too, and use a paper fastener to attach the arrow to the circle. Play with the arrow until it spins freely.

When you are ready to play, you and your child take turns writing lines to a good/bad story, except with this variation. The story will not progress in a perfect good/bad rotation. In this game, sadly enough, bad news may follow bad news and lead to even more bad news. If the characters are lucky, though, the story may move from one good news moment to another. In this game, bad luck and good luck are a matter of chance. This is because the spinner determines what type of line you have to write. If the arrow lands on *"That's good,"* you write a sentence about good news, and you add the all-important words: "That's good." If the arrow lands on *"That's bad,"* you write a sentence about bad news, followed by the words, "That's bad." If you land on *"That's good/That's bad,"* you must write a bit of good news followed by "That's good," and then a bit of bad news followed by "That's bad." You might prefer to reverse the order and begin with bad news, which is okay to do. If, however, the spinner lands on *"Lose a turn,"* the news is so bad that you don't get to write anything at all, and the other player gets to spin the spinner.

Sometimes, just for a change, you can vary the words "That's good" and "That's bad" with "That was good" and "That was bad," or "What good luck" and "What bad luck," or "Fortunately" and "Unfortunately."

Writing a THAT'S GOOD/THAT'S BAD story is fun by itself, but to keep the child's interest, you might want to keep score, too. Every line of good news gets five points. Every line of bad news gets three points. Good news and bad news written together count as eight points. "Lose a turn," of course, counts as no points at all.

Before you start a game, get a sheet of paper to use as a score card.

When you are ready to play your first game, go over the workings of a good/bad story with your child. Begin by reading the trip-to-the-zoo adventure that begins this activity. Then tell your child that the two of you will use the spinner to finish the story. Describe the scoring system and explain that each of you will take turns spinning. Then twirl the spinner and do as it tells you to do.

Record your score and then give the spinner to your child. The child spins, writes, and enters his points on the scorecard.

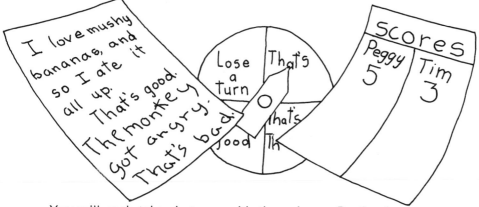

You will each take six turns with the spinner. By the time you are done, the story will surely have lurched through many goods and bads. But it won't have an ending. That's your next job.

You and your child each take a new sheet of paper, and you each compose an ending to the story. You mustn't write more than three sentences for the ending, and don't show each other your work until you are both finished. It doesn't matter if the ending is awkward, silly, or abrupt. You just need some reasonably viable way to conclude the story. Coming up with any ending at all—no matter how awful from a literary point of view—wins you six bonus points. If you develop a bad case of writer's block and can't think of a concluding thought, you miss out on this bonus. Assuming you both have managed to write an ending, you will have to pick which of the endings you prefer. Write that ending on the bottom of your good/bad tale—there's no additional bonus for the author of the better ending—and compute your scores. The player with the highest score wins.

Did you like the game? Then play again. You can start your second story from scratch, if you want. Or you can take a look on pages 80–81, where you will find six different beginnings to six different good/bad stories. Pick one you like. Read it to your child. Then get four fresh sheets of paper—one for writing the story, one for the scorecard, and two for writing the story endings.

This game may be a big hit in your house. That's good. Then again, your child may hate to play it. That's bad. Your child may enjoy himself anyway if, on adding up the points, you are forced to declare him the winner. That's good. You yourself might not like to lose. That's bad. Yet you might be pleased to see your child write so creatively. That's good. You might enjoy the creative challenge yourself. That's good, too. And if playing the game helps your child feel more at ease while writing, well, that's very good.

Six Good/Bad Beginnings

1. A Magic Ring

Jane was hungry for breakfast, but her favorite cereal box was empty. That's bad. She found a new box of cereal in her kitchen cabinet. That's good. The cereal didn't look right. That's bad. Jane looked closer and saw a ring in the box. That's good. The ring was ugly. That's bad. Suddenly the ring started to talk and said, "I'm a magic ring." That's good.

2. A Trip to the Circus

Tom and Gary went to the circus. That was good. They had to take their bratty little brother. That was bad. They saw the trapeze star. That was good. The bratty brother jumped into the circus ring and ran up to the clowns. That was bad.

3. A Treasure Map

Elizabeth found an old map in her grandmother's attic. That's good. The map was so old and dusty that Elizabeth couldn't make out any pictures or words on it. That's bad. She found a feather duster and cleaned the map. That's good. The writing on the map was very hard to read. That's bad. Using a magnifying glass, Elizabeth discovered that it was a pirate's map with directions to the pirate's buried treasure. That's good.

4. Hunting for Monsters

Clive thought he saw a monster in his bedroom closet. That's bad. He had a special monster-hunting kit under his bed. That's good. He was too frightened to climb out of bed and get the kit. That's bad.

5. Climbing a Mountain

Olivia is the world's greatest mountain climber. That's good. She was planning her biggest climbing trip when she hurt her foot playing soccer. That's bad. She decided to climb the mountain anyway, and she collected her gear. That's good. Halfway up the mountain she discovered that she had left her mountain-climbing rope behind. That's bad.

6. Fighting a Giant Python

Stacy and her twin sister, Tracy, were in the woods having a lovely picnic. That's good. Suddenly, they saw a creepy thing in the grass. That's bad. Stacy was scared, but Tracy said, "Don't worry. It's just a harmless little snake." That's good. Then Tracy got a closer look and saw a giant python beside the picnic basket! That's bad.

PART THREE

BUGABOOS— SPELLING, HANDWRITING, AND GRAMMAR

"It's a damn poor mind," President Andrew Jackson once wisely observed, "that can think of only one way to spell a word." Sew trew! Spelling is hell, and many a fine mind has suffered grievously because of it. John F. Kennedy was famous for having a bad back, but did you know that he had trouble spelling, too? The best authors can be the worst spellers. The original manuscript for F. Scott Fitzgerald's *The Great Gatsby* contained more than 5,000 spelling mistakes. Parents often worry that bad spelling by their own child may mean low intelligence. But that's not so. As we have seen, a bad speller might well become a president or a renowned novelist.

Quite often it's a good idea for parents and teachers to ignore the bad spelling that adorns children's papers, and in much of this book I advise parents and teachers to do just that. When adults fret about spelling, so do children. And when children worry about spelling, they often become nervous, inhibited writers. That will never do. Still, a child does eventually have to learn to spell. There is no getting around it. What if you found half a dozen spelling mistakes in this paragraph? You would probably take my ideas less seriously. Even worse, u mite haf trble figyouring owt whut I wunt tu seigh. Communication is the point of writing. You can't communicate accurately if your spelling is indecipherable.

Schools have always known this and have traditionally inflicted weekly spelling tests for the purpose of getting children to increase the number of words they can spell correctly and automatically. But those weekly tests, as has been confirmed by several educational research studies, have never been very effective. Parents know this firsthand. On Friday morning a child may get a perfect 100 percent score on a spelling quiz, but by Friday afternoon the same child may sit down to write a story and misspell word after word from his perfect test.

If weekly tests are not much use, how can you teach a child to spell? First and foremost, children should spend a lot of time reading and writing. Avid readers and enthusiastic writers tend to become competent spellers, F. Scott Fitzgerald's performance notwithstanding. Second, children should be given a lot of help in mastering the mysteries of phonetic sounds. Good spellers know how to listen for individual sounds in words, and they easily assign appropriate letters to represent those sounds. English spelling isn't all that phonetic, but phonetic skills do help. With a strong background in phonics, children can, indeed, spell many words they have never seen before. Third, children should learn to picture the way words look on the page. Think about the misspelled words you saw earlier in this discussion. Each word was phonetically accurate. *Ow* and *ou* make the same sound. But one glance at *owt* and you know it's wrong.

Finally, children should memorize how to spell the words they write most frequently. Unfortunately, many of the most common words in the English language are phonetically bewildering. Consider *was*, *said*, and *from.* If you sound out these words correctly according to the rules of phonics, you will spell them incorrectly: *wuz, sed, frum.* It's easy for beginning writers to get confused when spelling these words. The child who remembers *was* on Friday may revert to the sounded-out version, *wuz*, on Monday morning. The only solution to this problem is drill.

The prospect of drilling your child in spelling probably sounds extremely unappealing. But drill doesn't have to be painful. It can, in fact, be a game. In this section you'll find four games designed to provide painless spelling practice. Two of the games, WORD HUNT and SPEED CONTEST, help children remember how to spell words both for tests and for everyday writing. The game WHICH IS RIGHT? helps children remember the way words look when spelled correctly. Children who play ALPHABET CODE increase their knowledge of phonics. Unless your child already has an exceptional talent for spelling, these games won't turn him into a national spelling bee champion. But if you play them regularly, you will see results.

In addition to spelling, many children find that handwriting and grammar can also cause them considerable difficulty when they write. In first grade, children learn to print all the letters of the alphabet. By the end of second grade or the beginning of third, they learn to write in script. If you count both upper- and lowercase letters, children must learn four sets of alphabets in three years. This is an enormous task. Some children are blessed with dexterous fingers and a good memory for the shapes of letters. These children write legible words and don't require much instruction or practice to do so. Other children, just as intelligent, just as motivated, struggle with this chore. Try as they might, their compositions are only slightly more readable than a doctor's prescription.

When a child's handwriting is illegible—so much so that he can't read his own words—handwriting has become a problem that must be addressed. But why is this such a problem? If a child's handwriting is atrocious, why not just teach him to type? Computers, after all, are everywhere. Why, at the dawn of a new millennium, struggle with penmanship? It's true that someday computers may eliminate the need to write with pencil and paper. Perhaps future generations will talk into hand-held printers. This machine will instantly print out the spoken word in any font desired. But until then, the vast majority of children's written work will be done by hand, and so children must be able to produce understandable print, both in and out of school. If your child's handwriting could stand a little improvement, try playing WORDS BY DESIGN, TRAVELING WORDS, and DOTTED ALPHABET.

What about grammar? Which grammar lessons are appropriate for first-, second-, and third-graders? Children in these grades can and should be given some formal awareness of grammatical structure. They don't need to discuss direct objects or to diagram sentences, but they should realize that well-constructed sentences follow rules. *"Jimmy runs fast"* is a good sentence. *"Runs Jimmy fast"* is not—except, perhaps, in languages other than English. *"The red apple tastes sweet"* is a good sentence. *"The apple red tastes sweet"* is not. On an intuitive level, children know that subjects come before predicates and adjectives precede nouns. Without this knowledge a child wouldn't be able to speak. Intuitive knowledge is fallible, however, especially when it comes to writing. To nurture some knowledge of grammar is a good idea, then. Nurturing can begin early, if your approach is playful. There are just two grammar games in this section, MIXED-UP AND MISSING and STRANGE SENTENCES, but you can play these games again and again. They won't get boring, and they will help your child learn.

And remember that while some of the games in this section duplicate the procedures of classroom drill, the games are, in fact, games. If you aren't enjoying a particular activity, stop playing. Remember, too, that the mechanical aspects of writing—spelling, handwriting, and grammar—while important, are not the soul of writing. It is always more important to encourage children's love of composing stories than it is to perfect their skills in spelling or to refine their penmanship. Ironically, promoting a love of writing may be the best way to help children with mechanics, too. Because the more children like writing, the more they will write. And the more they write, the more skills they develop.

WORD HUNT

GRADES

first and second

MATERIALS

for beginners, photocopy the grid
on page 91
for advanced students,
photocopy the grid on page 92
a pencil
A List of Important Spelling
Words on pages 200–202

How does a typical first-grader spell the word *was*? *Wuz*, of course. How does this same youngster spell *of*? *Uv*, naturally. And the word *my*? *Mi* is often the first-grader's lettering of choice. Sound out these words for yourself and you will appreciate the logic. In order to spell, then, a child must overcome mere logic. There is only one way to accomplish this: practice, practice, practice.

Your child might like practicing with a WORD HUNT. To begin a WORD HUNT you should photocopy the grid on page 91, or else draw one for yourself. Then you should pick seven words from the lists on pages 200–202 and write them on a second sheet of paper. These lists are made up of the 370 words most commonly used in English. Children are supposed to know how to spell these words, if at all possible, by the time they finish third grade. The list is divided into three parts. There is an easy part, a tough part, and an even tougher part. I advise starting with words from the easy list.

Next copy the seven words onto the grid any old place you like, just so long as some of the words go horizontally and some go vertically.

Next, fill in all the blank spaces with random letters. Where did all those words go? They are hiding.

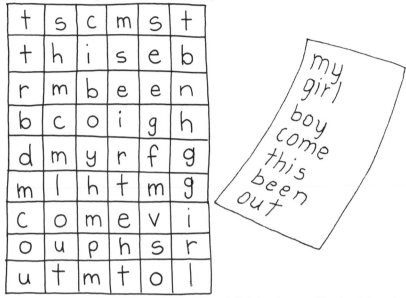

Now the game is ready. Give your child the letter-filled grid and the second sheet of paper with the seven words written down. Ask him to find the seven camouflaged words on the grid and circle them.

How does the child approach this daunting task? He hunts for one word at a time. He makes a chant of the letters in this word: "M-Y . . . M-Y . . . I have to find M-Y." Lo and behold, by the end of the game, the child is very likely to spell *my* correctly. The same will happen with *was* and *of.*

Children enjoy this game and are willing to play it repeatedly. Some children ask permission to create hunts for me. I whole-heartedly approve of this plan. In fact, I suggest playing a competitive version of this game. To do so, I make two copies of the blank grid and two copies of the hunt words. The child makes a hunt board for me while I make one for him. Then we exchange grids. The player who finds all seven words first wins the hunt. Adults have an advantage in this game. They are more familiar with the written form of the words and so they will spot the words more easily than children. To even the balance, you might give your child a sixty-second head start. You could also begin the hunt with your child and then secretly indulge in a little reverse cheating and slow yourself down.

You can make the hunt harder for more advanced students. Just use the grid on page 92 and increase the number of words from seven to twelve.

You'll find that WORD HUNTS can also come in handy when a child has to study for spelling tests. At homework time, make several grids and fill them in with spelling-test words. It's amazing how easily a WORD HUNT can transform an extremely onerous job of studying for a test into an enjoyable session of play. Your child may even beg for the chance to study in this way—which would be inconceivable if the study were a drill.

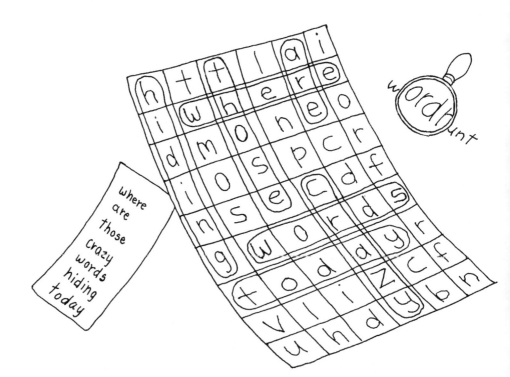

"*I* hate memorizing spelling words. It's so boring," Ginny complained.

As childhood grievances go, that's a pretty common one. And that is easily solved—not just with WORD HUNT but with this game, too: SPEED CONTEST. When engaged in a SPEED CONTEST, a child writes one word over and over again. If he can write the word enough times within a space of forty-five seconds, he wins the game.

To begin a SPEED CONTEST, you, the adult, pick a word that is hard for your child to spell. Write the word on the top of a sheet of paper.

GRADES

first, second, and third

MATERIALS

paper
pencil
stopwatch or any watch with a
second hand
A List of Important Spelling
Words on pages 200–202

Give your child a few moments to study the word. Meanwhile, get hold of a stopwatch or a watch with a second hand. When your child feels he has studied sufficiently, give him exactly forty-five seconds to write the word as many times as he can. He gets one point for each word he writes. He must avoid misspelling, however, since you will disqualify any mistakes. The words have to be reasonably legible, too, with every letter distinct. When the forty-five seconds pass, check your child's paper and award points.

Once you know your child's score, it's time for your own part in the contest. On a fresh sheet of paper, you will write the same word as your child. You will have the same forty-five seconds to copy the word and you will get the same one point per word.

But since you write more quickly than your child, you will surely get a higher score, which isn't fair—as any child will point out. Therefore, to win the game, the adult must more than *triple* the child's score. If your child writes the word ten times, you must write it more than thirty times. If your child writes the word twelve times, you must write it more than thirty-six times. Meet your triple-speed goal and you win the game. Fail and your child wins.

SPEED CONTEST is a simple game, but it works. It helps a child memorize the correct spelling of the contest word. How? By getting the child to copy the word over and over again. Sheer drill. Every teacher knows that children have to write words over and over; and every child dreads the task. But children do not dread SPEED CONTEST. They enjoy it—especially when they see you desperately attempt to top their score.

When you have a SPEED CONTEST at home, what words should you use? You can use ones from your child's weekly spelling tests. You can look at your child's writing and pick words that he regularly misspells. Or you can choose from the word lists on pages 200–202, which include the 370 most common words in English. The sooner your child masters these words the better, and some of them are not easy to learn. So take out a sheet of paper and a pencil. Get your watch ready. Set? Go!

*T*he difference between a bad speller and a good speller is that while both of them botch a few words from time to time, a good speller notices his errors. And when he catches a mistake, he will pause, scratch his head, and try to correct the problem.

My student Paul was an excellent speller. While writing a story about an intergalactic war, he wrote:

The arme tank went fast.

But he didn't like what he saw. He tried new letters:

armey

He studied this version for a moment but wasn't pleased. He tried again:

army

Happy at last, Paul went on with the story.

Poor spellers operate less efficiently. Here's what happened to Josh, a student with profound problems in spelling. Josh was writing about rabbits when he recorded this:

mi rabit ran awae ystrdy

He reread the sentence and was perfectly satisfied. Curious about his reaction, I decided to investigate.

"Josh, do you see any problems with your words?" I asked.

"What do you mean?" he asked in reply.

"Are all the words just the way you want them?"

"Oh," he mumbled, "I guess I spelled something wrong."

"Can you pick out any misspellings?"

Josh looked at his page. "This one?" he asked pointing to "mi."

Even with a teacher's prodding, Josh could barely find his mistakes. His sense of how the words should look was so weak that he couldn't correct himself the way Paul could.

WHICH IS RIGHT?

GRADES

first, second, and third

MATERIALS

paper
pencil
A List of Important Spelling
Words on pages 200–202

Paul was extraordinarily good at observing his spelling mistakes; Josh was exceptionally bad. Most children fall somewhere in between, and almost all can benefit from a bit of play in this area. Hence WHICH IS RIGHT?

You need a blank sheet of paper and a pencil. Take the paper and divide it into nine squares, like this:

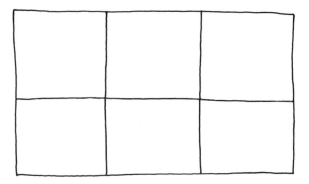

Each section represents a single round of the game, making nine rounds altogether. You play each round the same way. First you pick a word. Announce your choice to your child. Then write the word correctly along with two misspelled versions of the same word. You write the words one under the other with the properly spelled word in a different place each time. The misspellings should be pretty close to correct. If you pick the word *floor*, for instance, you might fill one section of the game board like this:

flor
floor
flore

The child studies these three words, and after thoughtful consideration, he picks the spelling that he thinks is right and draws a circle around it. If he is right, he gets two points. If he is wrong, you get two points. When a child makes a mistake on the first try, he gets a second go at the word. If he picks the right word on this next attempt, he gets one point. If he is wrong, you get one more point.

Then it's on to the next round. At the end of nine rounds, the player with the most points wins. If a child manages to win every round, I call that a grand-slam victory. If a child wins all but one round, I call that a mini-slam victory. With grand slams and mini-slams at stake, the game stays suspenseful even after a child wins eight out of eight rounds.

How does a student like Josh respond to this game? When Josh looks at *mi* in his own story, he feels perfectly content. But, if he had to choose the right spelling among *mi*, *my*, and *mu* he would probably select the correct version. And, having done this in a game, he will be more likely to write a proper *my* the next time he sits down to compose a story. You shouldn't look for miraculous progress in spelling as a result of playing a single game. But a gradual and unmiraculous progress is certainly within reach.

You can use any words at all for a game of WHICH IS RIGHT? You may want to play the game to help your child master the word lists on pages 200–202, for instance. Or you might want to select words from the dictionary or a children's book. You can also use "adult" words selected from a newspaper, magazine, or a book from your own shelf.

Kids enjoy WHICH IS RIGHT?—at least many of them do. Will your child enjoy it, too? It will take you only a few minutes to find out. Give it a try one evening while waiting for spaghetti water to boil; by dinner time you'll know.

ALPHABET CODE

GRADES

second and third

MATERIALS

paper
pencil

*T*ake a common word, such as *tiger*, and carefully rearrange the letters in alphabetical order. The result is:

egirt

Egirt is *tiger* in alphabet code. Write *egirt* on a sheet of paper and hand it to your child. Challenge him to crack your alphabet code and figure out the original word.

There are two ways a child can unjumble the mixed-up word. He can randomly arrange the letters this way and that, hoping that a familiar word will appear. Or he can think logically about the letter combinations that are most typically seen in English. Either way is legitimate, but the second approach, the logical one, has definite advantages.

If you look at the letters *e-g-i-r-t* logically, certain letter combinations are bound to seem more promising than others. It's hard, for instance, to think of very many words that contain the *tg* combination. A *tg* appears in words like *mortgage* and *nightgown*, but not in too many others.

On the other hand, you do see *gr* together all the time, especially at the beginning of words. Might not *gr* come at the beginning of the mystery word that lurks with the encoded *egirt*? It's worth trying out some possibilities:

greit   griet   grite   greti

Too bad; none of these are words. What about *tr*? *Tr* is another blend commonly seen at the beginning of words. A *tr* beginning yields these possibilities:

treig   trieg   trige   tregi

Nothing yet. What about *er*? Er is a popular combination. Sometimes it starts a word.

ergit   ertig   ertig

Often it ends a word.

giter   tiger

Yes! That's it:

tiger!

I play this game with children because I want to help them gain some sense of spelling logic. Of course, I don't expect a child to decode words with the kind of sophistication that an adult might bring to bear. Instead, I give the child a word—for instance, *trip*—properly encoded:

iprt

And I let the child consider the letters. Sometimes I give a hint, "I see two possible beginning blends: *pr* and *tr.* You could give one a try." Given enough helpful suggestions, children usually manage to solve the puzzle.

Children often like to turn the tables and encode their own word. They jumble the letters (that is, put them in alphabetical order) and challenge me to solve the puzzle. I'm always happy to comply. I set about the task, and all the while I think out loud. I chatter away, detailing my ideas about spelling, letter combinations, proper use of blends, and so on.

ALPHABET CODE is a good game for a rainy Saturday. Sit your child down. Teach him the rules, which are simple enough. Coach him to victory on his first effort, and very likely the child will want to play again. ALPHABET CODE is also a game that children might want to play with each other, even without an adult.

You can use any words at all for this game. But you might as well take advantage of the following list. It has twenty words that will challenge without frustrating most second- and third-graders.

cap	pass	ripe	clean
run	rack	maze	dream
fin	trip	track	right
mix	left	smoke	school
fill	cape	boat	banana

There is one other rule in this game. Let's say your secret word is *stop* and your child unjumbles the letters to discover *post* or *pots.* In this case, you declare the child a winner. Any word that exists in the English language is good enough to win a round of ALPHABET CODE.

WORDS BY DESIGN is an unusual but effective way to improve your child's penmanship. It's hard, when you are six or seven years old, to memorize the shapes of all the letters. It's no easy matter to control the small muscles in your hand, but it's important to learn to do so if you want to produce well-formed letters. How dreary it is to practice drawing the letters over and over. Here's a way to make the practice fun. Have your child begin by writing a single word in a light pencil stroke. Encourage him to use his best handwriting.

GRADES

first, second, and third

MATERIALS

paper
pencil
crayons or colored pencils

Then tell him to go back over the letters, using colored pencils and drawing little designs. He can draw diamonds, spirals, ovals, squares, or dots. Each letter or design can be in a new color.

Your child might like to use this kind of writing to make birthday cards, welcome-home banners, and signs that say KEEP OUT OF MY ROOM! It can be amusing for a child to write in this style, yet it is also useful. For by going over and over each letter with the colored pencils in order to make complicated designs, the child is giving himself practice in making the correct shapes for letters and controlling his hand.

A child who is learning script can still design words. Begin with a word or a short sentence in script and then ornament it with colorful shapes.

TRAVELING WORDS

GRADES

first, second, and third

MATERIALS

paper
pencil
colored pencils

*H*ere's another way to turn the monotony of handwriting practice into something a child might actually want to do. Pick a sentence for your child to write—a weird or funny sentence preferably, something that might elicit a laugh. For instance: *That giant ate a million worms for dinner.* Normally you would write this sentence in a straight line. But things aren't normal in this game. Your next job is to draw a road, a winding road, and on this road your child should inscribe the weird sentence. The road might look like this:

or this:

or this:

And after your child writes this sentence as neatly as possible, the road should look like this:

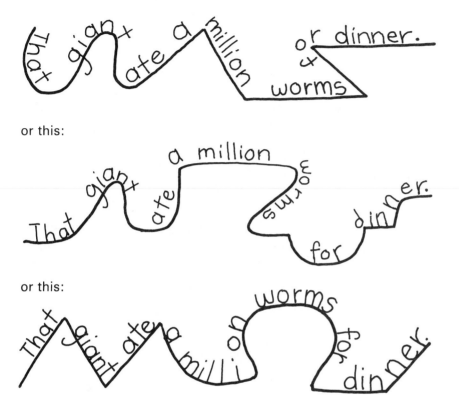

or this:

or this:

If your child is learning script, it might be a good idea to travel down the road in cursive letters.

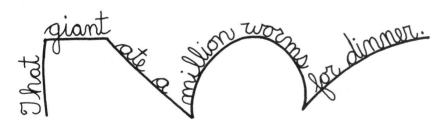

Here's a collection of sentences you can use on days when inventing your own is too much effort.

Bees buzz in big baskets.
Is that a cow I see swimming in the sea?
Live lizards live in Larry's locker.
I cry when I spy a hairy scary spider eye.
My jolly jellyfish is stuck in orange marmalade!
That crazy fox fixed cornflakes for a wild wolf.
Who sells seashells by Peter Piper's pickle store?
Flying fish swiped my five fresh fruit pies.
Wicked witches like watching mean monsters smash
  vile villains.
A billion bubbles floated over the ginger ale ocean.

Play this game as often as you and your child like. Good penmanship comes from rigorous practice, and the practice that comes from playing TRAVELING WORDS is more rigorous than you may think.

One day, I turned to Sophie, a third-grader, and said, "Here's a way to practice handwriting that's lots of fun. It's called DOTTED ALPHABET. In this game, you make all of your letters out of dots. Here's how *Sophie* looks in DOTTED ALPHABET."

"That's pretty," she said.
"Thank you," I replied.
I told Sophie that there are two ways to make dotted letters— the Easy Way and the Hard Way. You begin the Easy Way by writing a letter very neatly using a light pencil stroke.

Sophie

Then you take a pen or a colored pencil and trace your way over the letter with dots.

Sophie

To make a dotted letter the Hard Way, you don't begin with a pencil stroke. Instead, you plunge in with dots. Dot, dot, dot, and soon enough you have a letter.

GRADES

first, second, and third

MATERIALS

paper
pencil

To use the Hard Way with success, the DOTTED ALPHABET writer has to command a deep and decisive knowledge of letter shapes. Any uncertainty about which way a letter should go will result in an extravagance of lopsidedness.

You can write in dotted script, too. It can be done the Easy Way. Write the whole word in script and then start dotting.

Or do it the Hard Way—nothing but dots.

You can write in dotted script, too. It can be done the Easy Way. Write the whole word in script and then start dotting.

Sophie liked this new game. It was an entertaining way to play with penmanship. Will DOTTED ALPHABET be a success in your house? Who knows? It could well be a

*T*here's no reason for first-, second-, and third-graders to memorize the rules of grammar. But young children do need to develop a good ear for language and a firm intuitive sense of what makes a good sentence. A child who gains a sophisticated intuitive feeling about sentence structure from an early age will usually find it easy to cope with the formal rules of grammar when the time comes.

MIXED-UP AND MISSING is a good game for getting children to develop an ear for sentence structure. I began playing it with Rebecca by telling her to cover her eyes. Then I wrote a simple sentence on a sheet of paper:

GRADES

first, second, and third

MATERIALS

paper
pencil
scissors

I cut out each word . . .

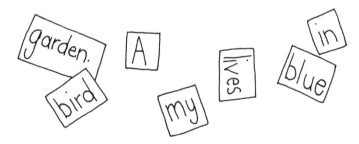

and mixed them all up.

"Open your eyes," I said. "What do you see?"
"Lots of words," she answered.
"True, but these aren't stray words. If you put them together in the right order, you'll get a sentence. That's your job. Take the

mixed-up sentence and fix it up. Do you think you can?" I asked.
She nodded.

"I'll give you two hints," I said. "Remember, every sentence starts with a capital letter. And every sentence ends with a punctuation mark: either a period, an exclamation point, or a question mark. If you think about that, you can figure out where to place two of the words."

"I get it," Rebecca declared as she moved the words around. She set up the first and last words.

Now Rebecca had some thinking to do. She had to consider the structure of sentences. This sentence begins with the word *A.* Logically, Rebecca had to wonder "A what?" You don't have *A my* or *A lives.* But *A bird* makes sense. So it seemed to Rebecca, and that gave her the second word of the sentence.

What does a bird do? That's what a proper English sentence should tell you next. Rebecca knew that a bird doesn't *in* or *my.* A bird *lives,* however.

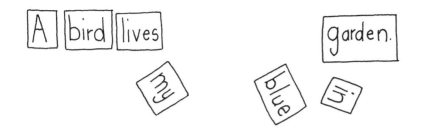

With these words in place, Rebecca shouted, "I've got it!" She quickly added two more words.

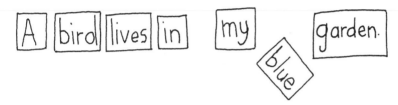

"But there's still a word that doesn't fit," she complained.

"Where can that *blue* go? What could be blue?" I asked.

Rebecca understood that only things can be blue. There were only two things in the sentence: the bird and the garden.

"It can't be a blue garden," she said with a giggle. "It must be a blue bird."

"Hooray for you," I cheered.

I was truly delighted. By putting this one sentence together, Rebecca had given thought to the grammatical foundations of not just this one sentence but of every sentence. She didn't know it, but she had just had a grammar lesson.

I was ready to play a second round but Rebecca interrupted. It was her turn now, she said, to write a sentence, cut it up, and watch me struggle to put it back in order. I agreed to this arrangement. It was hard for Rebecca to think of something to write, though. So I gave her a children's book and suggested she copy a sentence. She picked a long one and it took her several minutes to copy all the words onto a sheet of paper and cut them out. It took me even longer to reposition them.

Rebecca liked this game, and I enjoyed playing with her. After a few rounds, however, I introduced a harder version of MIXED-UP AND MISSING. The harder version begins just like the easier one. Again I told Rebecca to cover her eyes while I wrote a simple sentence on a sheet of paper:

I cut out each of the words.

But this time I took one word and hid it in my pocket.

I shuffled the remaining words, put them on the table, and told Rebecca to open her eyes.

Now Rebecca had two jobs. First, she had to rearrange the words into a meaningful sentence. But since one word was missing, that was a much harder job than before. Still, some things are eternal, and among them are the rules of grammar. The first word of a sentence always begins with a capital letter and the last word is invariably followed by a period, an exclamation point, or a question mark. Relying on these unfailing rules, she selected the first and last words of the sentence.

My is usually followed by a person or an object: my boat, my computer, my friend. So Rebecca had to look for a person or object among the words. How about *My ice* or *My vanilla*? Those were possibilities. Knowing the action of the sentence might help. What would the *ice* or *vanilla* do? They would have to lick. *My ice licks cream*? Wait a minute: *ice* and *cream* are words that often go together. Wait again: it could be *vanilla ice cream*! The sentence might be (and here Rebecca took a guess): *My vanilla ice cream licks*. That didn't seem right. Another possibility was *My licks vanilla ice cream*. Now it was fairly obvious that the missing word had to identify who or what happens to like ice cream. The sentence had to be: *My* (something-or-other) *licks vanilla ice cream*. But what could that be?

It was time for me to offer hints, and for her to guess.

"It's got claws," I said.

"Claws? It could be a cat. It could be a dog. It's not a mouse, I'm positive. Is it a cat?" she asked.

"Yes," I said. "You're amazing! I didn't think you would guess my word."

"Now I get to write a sentence for you, right?" asked Rebecca. "I'm going to make it hard, too," she added with a mischievous grin.

Not all children like the missing-word version of this game. Some children find it too difficult. If that's the case with your child, go back to the simpler mixed-up game, without a missing word.

Remember, you want your child to succeed more often than fail when he plays. If he's successful, he'll want to play again. Don't, therefore, insist that he discover your exact original sentence. If he turns *The circus clown rode a camel* into *The clown rode a circus camel*, consider that a victory. After all, it's plausible and it's good English.

Here's a list of twenty sentences you and your child might use for this game.

His hamster hid in my shoe.
That mean dog barked at me.
Did you see a red balloon?
Baby bear ate all the honey.
A lion lives in that cave!
My best friend is so silly.
I will never eat liver!
Can you walk on your hands?
That bird made a loud noise.
She loves to play baseball.
My brother took my bike.
The princess lost her gold ring.
A pirate buried all his treasure here.
Throw the ball to first base.
My sister caught a firefly.
I don't want to go to bed.
Let's take a trip to the zoo.
He drew a beautiful picture.
You can't play with my puppy.
I lost a tooth this afternoon.

There is no reason not to invent your own sentences. Just keep them simple, without too many adjectives or adverbs.

*T*he other day, I overheard a pair of four-year-olds gibbering nonsense. One child blurted, "Glumish, fudticle moompoo!" and then both children dissolved into giggles. Delighted with themselves, they continued their conversation. Nonsense appeals to children. Of course, as they get older they demand more sophisticated silliness. That's the appeal of STRANGE SENTENCES. It gives children the opportunity to compose nonsensical sentences. The game should appeal to you, too, because it helps your child understand the grammatical anatomy of common sentences.

You need one playing die and a STRANGE SENTENCES chart. Here's the chart:

GRADES

first, second, and third

MATERIALS

paper
pencil
one playing die
game chart
markers, stapler

	WHO or WHAT	DID WHAT	WHERE	WHEN	. or !
1.	A spider	ate a fly	in a web	at midnight	.
2.	The president	got angry	in the White House	Halloween night	!
3.	A polar bear	ate raw fish	on an iceberg	in January	!
4.	A robot	lost a part	on a spaceship	during lunch	.
5.	My cat	chased a mouse	in the barn	this morning	!
6.	A rock star	sang a song	on television	last night	.

You can copy the chart onto a sheet of paper or keep the book open to this page as you play. You'll also need a sheet of paper to record your sentences.

To begin, you must determine the subject of your sentence—the "who or what." This you decide by rolling the die. Let's say you get a three. Look on the chart under WHO OR WHAT. In the third row you'll see *A polar bear.* That means your sentence will start with the words *A polar bear.* Write these words on a sheet of paper.

A polar bear

Now you must determine what your subject, the polar bear, has done. Roll again. Let's say you get a six. Look at the chart under DID WHAT. Find the sixth row in this column and you'll see the words *sang a song.* Write *sang a song* after *A polar bear.* Clearly, the nonsense is taking shape.

Now move to the next column, WHERE. Roll the die to find out exactly *where* the polar bear sang a song. A four? It was on a spaceship (as you will see by consulting the chart). Roll again in order to find out when the bear did his singing. You got another four? According to the chart the bear burst into song during lunch.

You must roll the die once more. This time you'll find out whether your sentence is a statement or an exclamation. Let's say you roll a five. Look in the far-right-hand column, the one with the final punctuation. The fifth row has an exclamation mark. After you finish writing the results of this last roll of the die, your entire sentence will look like this:

A polar bear sang a song

on a spaceship during lunch!

Sentences such as this have the power to send many children into irrepressible giggle fits, which is fine and should encourage the child to take the die in hand and roll it enough times to create still more STRANGE SENTENCES.

Some children enjoy illustrating these sentences after they have written them down. Yvonne, a talented second-grader, rolled the die to produce a sentence, and then illustrated it:

She illustrated some other sentences, too, and eventually we had a ten-page collection of beautiful nonsensical sentences. I made a cover page and we stapled the sheets together into a *Strange Sentences Book.*

Of course, you can change the game chart any time you want. Here's a list of possible whos, whats, wheres, and whens you can substitute for the ones above. You might have some even wilder ideas. If so, go ahead, stick them in. Inventing new combinations is a perfect way to keep this game interesting.

	WHO or WHAT	DID WHAT	WHERE	WHEN	. or !
1.	My dad	baked a pie	in the kitchen	yesterday	.
2.	A dinosaur	lived	in a lake	millions of years ago	!
3.	My friend	hid	under the bed	today	!
4.	A goldfish	swam	in a fish tank	all night	.
5.	A frog	swallowed a fly	in a swamp	at dawn	!
6.	My grandfather	read a book	on a sofa	this morning	.

My dad read a book in a fish tank at dawn.

As children play this game, they become familiar with the four W's: who, what, where, and when. The W's make up the basic structure of a huge percentage of the sentences that children read and write. Understanding how the W's work in sentences is, therefore, very important. So play a little, giggle a little, and know that as you do so your child is learning more than a little about English grammar.

PART FOUR
WRITING WITH STYLE

It's impossible to teach someone to be a Shakespeare. Even Shakespeare couldn't do it. But to teach children to write intelligently and interestingly at a sub-Shakespearian level is entirely possible. The structure of well-told stories, the logical ordering of ideas, the creating of vivid images and of memorable characters, the principles of prose style—all these are difficult to learn, but there is no mystery about them. Children can acquire quite a few of these skills, and they can do it by playing games. You will find eight amusing games in this section, each one of which will teach your child some aspect of the skill and knowledge that go into writing intelligently and well.

SHE IS SO MEAN and WHAT A PERSONALITY encourage children to imagine vivid characters by playing a board game and composing truly nasty stories, which are always fun to write. HOW MANY WORDS? is an exciting dice game that inspires children to use precise and evocative language in their writing. FORBIDDEN LETTERS helps children develop a larger and more varied vocabulary, which is important for any kind of writer. EGG-CARTON TALES and WRITING TO FORM will help your child learn to write more logically and to follow the established forms of storytelling. THE THREE-SENTENCE CHALLENGE helps children summarize and organize information which, in turn, helps young authors write clear, concise prose. I'M A QUIET MOUSE encourages children to be imaginative in their use of language. All children can benefit by playing these games—good writers, not-so-good writers, new writers, and writers with a bit of experience. You may find that the games can help adult writers, too.

Zach, a second-grader, loved writing action-filled war stories. When it came to describing gruesome combat and ferocious battles, Zach was a master. He didn't show much interest in characters, however. The people in his stories threw bombs and navigated fighter jets, but they didn't talk or think or feel. As a result, Zach's stories were exciting but they lacked a human dimension.

There was no point in urging Zach to imagine what kind of individuals his warriors might be. I needed a more playful approach. When it comes to helping a child create characters, nothing is more effective than writing a SHE IS SO MEAN story.

Here is how it works. "A SHE IS SO MEAN story," I told Zach, "is a story starring the meanest, nastiest, most rotten and miserable person we can imagine. We take turns writing about this wretched person. I start by writing down some mean vile thing the person does. Then you outdo me—if you can."

I knew the challenge would appeal to Zach.

I took up a pencil and wrote:

> I know the meanest person in the world. She is so mean, she once sneaked into a kindergarten class and broke all the toys.

Zach laughed. "I like that," he said.

"Thanks," I answered, "I'm proud of it myself. Can you imagine anything meaner?"

He grabbed the pencil and, just below my contribution, wrote:

> She is so mean she makes her dog eat rotten eggs.

GRADES

first, second, and third

MATERIALS

paper
pencil
colored pencils or markers

"That's mean," I said. "That's *really* mean. It will be hard to dream up a nastier idea, but I'll try." I considered several possibilities before writing:

She is so mean, she never smiles. She hasn't smiled in 10 years. Her face is so disgusting that when she looks in a mirror, the mirror smashes to smithereens.

We each contributed three more wicked thoughts and then declared our character study complete. We added a few drawings to the page. They were almost as unusual as the story.

Zach found every disgusting thought and illustration perfectly delightful.

During our next work session, we wrote a new story. It featured the silliest man in the world. This man is so silly, he eats dinner standing on his head. He is so silly, he visits the North Pole in January wearing a bathing suit. He is so silly, he uses shoes for earmuffs. What a guy!

Over the next several weeks, Zach and I wrote many character studies. Here are some of our most successful titles:

He Is So Loud	*She Is So Lazy*	*He Is So Fast*
She Is So Strong	*He Is So Confused*	*She Is So Smart*
He Is So Mysterious	*She Is So Dirty*	*He Is So Hungry*

Zach enjoyed writing these stories, but I must concede, his other writing didn't change as a result. The moment had come for more pointed and aggressive action. Zach was writing a story about evil aliens intent on taking over the Earth. He called his aliens Splufluxians and the story was crammed with action. He hadn't managed to describe a single alien, however.

After reading the story and congratulating Zach on his thrilling plot, I broached the subject of characters.

"I bet there's a head Splufluxian. I bet he's really nasty. I'd love to know more about him. Do you think you could tell me more? Can you describe some of his meanness?"

In the past, Zach had refused to make any changes in his stories. This time, though, he thought for a moment and said, "I want the head Splufluxian to be so mean he eats live rats for dinner. And his name is . . ." Zach paused to think. "Roloove."

"He eats live rats! That gives me goose bumps," I said with a shiver.

Zach smiled shyly. We scanned his story until we found a spot to include his horrifying idea. Then he carefully wrote down the new and ghastly details about Roloove, the head Splufluxian.

This marked a major change in Zach's writing. He was now willing, even eager, to develop interesting characters. Soon his imagined personalities were as complex as his dynamic plots, which signified wonderful, and very satisfying, progress in his writing.

WHAT A PERSONALITY

GRADES

second and third

MATERIALS

two game sheets from page 126
pencils
index cards
scissors

When Honoré de Balzac lay on his deathbed, he surprised his visitors—so it is said—by asking them to summon Dr. Bianchon to his side. Dr. Bianchon was a medical savant who had aided many a sickly person—though only in Balzac's novels. For he was Balzac's own creation; in real life the doctor didn't exist. Such is the imagination of a great writer. The fictional world can be more real than reality.

To learn to write well, a child needs to become a bit like Balzac in this regard. A child needs to learn how to imagine make-believe people and things with the vividness of life, and how to get those imaginings down on paper. Writing a SHE IS SO MEAN story is one way to help children create interesting characters. WHAT A PERSONALITY is another.

To begin a WHAT A PERSONALITY game, you need pencils, game sheets, and special playing cards. These playing cards are easy to make. Take eight index cards and cut them into fourths, which gives you thirty-two small cards. On two of those cards, write the word SORRY. On fifteen other cards, write the numbers one through fifteen, then one through fifteen yet again on the remaining cards.

The model for your game sheet is on page 126. It is composed of fifteen squares, each one containing an unfinished sentence. Square ten, for instance, says: *My character's favorite food is ___.* Square fourteen says: *Someday my character would like to ___.* You need to make two copies of this sheet, one for yourself and one for your child. You can draw your own sheets or you can make photocopies from the book—perhaps several copies, in case you want to play the game several times or with more than one child, which is always possible.

Once you have prepared the cards and the game sheets, you're ready to play. Spread out the cards face down on the table. Now comes the crucial part. You must pick a character from books or movies or TV or real life, and your child must pick a different character. Here are some possibilities: Cinderella, Bart Simpson, the Wicked Witch of the West, the Big Bad Wolf, Jack the Giant Killer, Jackie Robinson, George Washington.

Let's say you choose Cinderella and your child chooses the Big

Bad Wolf. Now you take turns picking cards. Your first card happens to be, say, an eight. Square eight of the game sheet reads: *My character laughs when ___.* You have to fill in the blank. When, exactly, does Cinderella laugh? Perhaps when she dances. So you complete the sentence by writing: "she dances." Then you remove the card from the field of play.

Now your child picks a card—let's say it's a seven. The child reads aloud from square seven, which is: *My character's favorite color is ___.* The child has to select a favorite color for the Big Bad Wolf. Don't be surprised if your child is stumped by this question. Anybody could be stumped by such a question. Yet the point of the game is to try to picture the Big Bad Wolf's personality; and since everybody, according to one theory of personality, has a favorite color, so must the Big Bad Wolf, and your child must decide what it is. A little help or encouragement from you might be in order here.

"What *would* the Big Bad Wolf like as his favorite color?" you might ask. "Perhaps pink—the color of raw meat? What do you think?" If your child agrees, the child writes "pink" in square seven. Then the child removes card number seven from the table. And it is now your turn again to pick a card. Don't hesitate to ask your child for help when you are stumped. "What does Cinderella like to do on Saturday?" you may ask. "Visit her fairy godmother," announces your child. Yes, that sounds good, and so you get to fill in another square.

Since there are two sets of numbers, one through fifteen, you could easily pick a number that you have already used. If that happens, you lose your turn and you must turn the card face down and return it to the rest of the unpicked cards. Alternatively, you might pick one of the two cards that say SORRY. If that happens, sorry, but in this case, too, you lose your turn. And you must let the SORRY card rejoin the unpicked cards so that it can continue to plague both you and your child.

That's all there is to WHAT A PERSONALITY. You and your child take turns picking cards and completing sentences. In about fifteen minutes one player will finish writing all of the sentences and, therefore, win the game.

You may find it fun to invite more people to join the game. Three, four, five, or even six people could have a perfectly good time playing WHAT A PERSONALITY. But you will have to make enough copies of the game sheet and prepare more playing cards, too—make one SORRY card and fifteen numbered cards per player.

WHAT A PERSONALITY is not guaranteed to turn your child into a Balzac. But it is sure to help your child begin to imagine fictional characters in more vivid ways, which is a good thing for any writer.

Game Sheet

1. My character's name is

_____

2. My character is _____ years old.

3. My character lives

_____ .

4. My character's hair color is

_____

5. My character's eyes are

_____

6. My character's favorite time of year is

_____

7. My character's favorite color is

_____

8. My character laughs when

_____

9. My character gets angry when

_____

10. My character's favorite food is

_____

11. My character would like to own

_____

12. My character loves it when

_____

13. On Saturday my character likes to

_____

14. Someday my character would like to

_____

15. My character's favorite kind of music is

_____

*T*he following two sentences describe the same event:

The dog jumped over the fence.

The ferocious dog jumped over the wooden fence.

GRADES

first, second, and third

MATERIALS

the word chart on page 129
one playing die
masking tape
paper
pencil
pen

The first sentence gives you the unadorned facts. The second sentence gives you, in addition, a couple of vivid details. Young children, when they begin to write, usually stick to simple sentences and unadorned facts, and for good reason, too. Young children tend to write the way they speak; and since in talking about a dog and a fence a child will usually speak in simple sentences, his written version will tend to be the same.

Children do admire a more descriptive language, though, and with adult help they are happy to sprinkle their sentences with colorful adjectives and adverbs and details of every kind. HOW MANY WORDS? is an easy and yet effective way to give that help.

You need the chart of colorful words located at the end of the game, a pencil, a pen, and a playing die, which you must modify with a bit of masking tape. Over the face of the die that shows six dots, put a tiny piece of tape and mark two dots on it with a pen. Another bit of tape goes over the five-dot face, and there you should draw three dots. You should now have a die with faces numbered 1, 2, 2, 3, 3, and 4.

You and your child take turns during this game. Let's say that you begin. You roll the die and get a three. Look at the first three words on the word chart: *kitten, horrible, delightful.* You want to include as many of these words as you can in a single sentence. If you use all three words, you get three points.

The delightful kitten didn't want to eat his horrible dinner.

If you can't think of a way to use all three words, you can use just two of the words and get two points.

The kitten hated the horrible dog.

Perhaps it's the end of a long, hard day and you can't squeeze more than one chart word into a sentence.

I love my kitten.

Then you get just one point.

Now it's your child's turn. Give him the die and let him roll. If he gets a three, he, too, takes three words from the chart, but not by starting at the top. Instead he begins where you left off: *grasshopper, sleepy, loudly.* Assure your child that spelling and penmanship don't count in this game. Writing a coherent and grammatically correct sentence does, however. *The grasshopper sleepy ate* won't do. Nor will *The grasshopper ate sleepy. The sleepy grasshopper ate a cookie* is a fine sentence, however, and will win two points.

Play as many rounds as you want. When you're done, whoever has the most points wins the game.

Almost every sentence produced by you or your child while playing this game will include an adjective or an adverb. Consequently, by playing, your child will get accustomed to using such words. The more you play, the more accustomed he will be, which is to the good.

If you want to try a more challenging version of the game, don't tape over the numbers five and six. With five and six showing you will have the opportunity to rack up more points, but you'll have to cope with as many as five or six words in order to do so.

There are 200 words on the chart. That should be enough for several games. When you get to the end, you can start again from the beginning or rewrite the chart in a new order. Better yet, make your own chart. Spend a few minutes with your child thinking up unusual words. You could pluck a few words out of a dictionary or a thesaurus and incorporate them into the chart, just to add an exotic touch. And there's no reason why the child should already know the meaning of every new word you put on the list. HOW MANY WORDS? is mostly about adjectives and adverbs but it also provides some opportunity to introduce your child to new vocabulary words.

A Chart of Colorful Words

kitten	cute	yellow	horse
horrible	thin	swiftly	purplish
delightful	magical	canary	puppy
grasshopper	quickly	stroll	crimson
sleepy	clean	milk	speedy
loudly	silly	hard	softly
tasty	grass	itchy	teeth
race	carefully	mean	kind
dirty	mountain	hairy	smelly
fly	messy	president	call
slowly	telephone	busy	dark
free	helpful	harmful	juicy
awful	terrific	quietly	hungry
sadly	tight	balloon	roses
mad	curly	twist	huge
French fries	sour	sweetly	ugly
sunny	splendid	pencil	mouse
watch	swing	slide	golden
silky	bright	calmly	angrily
sticky	special	noodle	loose
giant	elf	mushy	truck
dangerous	safely	shout	lost
marshmallow	lucky	rotten	bloody
boring	long	skinny	tomato
computer	rich	furry	empty

FORBIDDEN LETTERS

GRADES

second and third

MATERIALS

one playing die
masking tape
paper
pencil
pen

*T*here was once a French writer named Georges Perec who wrote a whole book, *La Disparition*, without ever using the letter *e*. Every time he wanted to write a word with an *e*, he had to search his mind for an *e*-less synonym. Obviously, Perec had a phenomenal vocabulary. Exactly why Perec submitted himself to such a ridiculous rule, I cannot say. But his idea of writing without a particular letter does pose a challenge that can be amusing and instructive for children. Here's a game based on Perec's idea. It encourages children to employ a more varied vocabulary as they write.

Before you play, you must alter a playing die. Simply put little squares of masking tape over all six faces of the die. Then with a pen write letters on each piece of tape. For your first game, put the following six letters on the die, one on each face: *c, y, u, k, j,* and *g.*

Now roll the die. The letter you roll will be off limits to you for the duration of the game. You will write quite a bit during the game, but your forbidden letter may not appear in any of your words. Your child may use your forbidden letter when he writes, however. Of course he will also have a forbidden letter which he must studiously avoid using. He will discover this letter the same way you did, by rolling the die. If he rolls the same letter you did, then you must both avoid the *same* letter for the entire game.

What will you write? Begin a question-and-answer round-robin. You write a question for your child to answer—remembering, of course, to avoid your forbidden letter. Your child answers your question while avoiding his own forbidden letter. That is half a round in the game. Then your child writes a question for you, still avoiding his letter. You answer his question. That's the second half of a round. The game goes on for six rounds.

What happens if someone uses his forbidden letter? The game is over and the erring person has lost. If both players avoid their letters for all six rounds, you have a tie. In this game, if a child can manage a tie, I call him the winner. That means in order to win, I must make my young opponent write his prohibited letter. The child has two ways to win. He can make me use my forbidden letter or he can hold out for the full six rounds. Either way, victory will be his.

Once, while playing with Austin, a third-grader, I rolled a *c.* That meant no *c*ows, *c*amels, or wit*c*hes for me. Austin rolled a *g.*

I composed this question to start the game:

Where do people park
their automobiles?

I couldn't write "Where do people park their cars?" for the obvious reason that *c* was forbidden to me. But my question left Austin with a problem. He couldn't respond, "In the garage," or "In a parking lot," although these were the most logical answers. He had to think of a *g*-less parking place. It didn't take him long to solve this problem:

on the street

His answer was not a complete sentence, but there was no reason for it to be. Now he got to write a question for me to answer.

What animal purs?

Austin wrote *purs* instead of *purrs,* but I didn't mention his spelling mistake. I could read the word, and proper spelling isn't the point of this game. Besides, I had my own troubles. I had to answer his question. I couldn't write, "A cat." I needed a new word. I considered the problem and came up with a perfect response.

And so went the game.

Austin didn't know it, but this game has a significant educational purpose. It helps players learn to think flexibly about words. Good writers know that there is always more than one way to express an idea, and to find the *perfect* way to do it sometimes involves a strenuous mental search. Or should I say, the *ideal* word to express an idea? Maybe I should say, the *optimal* way. There are always alternatives, and FORBIDDEN LETTERS is a game that gets children to see many different possibilities.

A week after our first game, Austin and I played FORBIDDEN LETTERS again. This time, though, I changed the letters on the die and, in this way, increased the difficulty of the game. Some letters are harder to avoid than others. *E*, being the most commonly used letter, is the hardest of all to avoid. I don't imagine a game would last very long if one of the players was forced to avoid an *e*, unless somebody as wordily brilliant as Perec were the player. On the other hand, it's fairly easy to avoid an *x*. To make the game more challenging for Austin, I taped the letters *f, g, m, o, i,* and *s* to the die. Sidestepping any of these letters for long can cause anyone's head to pound.

When you play at home, you can pick your preferred level of difficulty. Below, you will find six sets of letters. The first set has fairly easy-to-avoid letters. The letters in the second set are harder to avoid. Go with the fourth set, as I did with Austin, and you and your child may find yourselves moaning and groaning your way through the game. You can, of course, pick your own letters. Any half-dozen of the twenty-six alphabet letters will do.

Easy Letters: z   x   w   q   j   v

Less Easy Letters: h   k   l   p   c   r

Somewhat Easy Letters: u   d   m   b   c   n

Somewhat Hard Letters: f   g   m   o   i   s

Hard Letters: s   a   m   n   t   i

Very Hard Letters: e   s   a   t   m   b

EGG-CARTON TALES

GRADES

first, second, and third

MATERIALS

two styrofoam egg cartons
one dime
paper
pencil
tape
scissors

*H*ow many stories have been told or written throughout the ages? Millions? Billions? Each one of these tales is different in some way from all the other stories. Yet virtually all stories, even the most unusual of them, have certain qualities in common. Every story takes place in a specific setting. All stories are populated by characters. Most stories have one or two main characters and several minor ones. The major characters usually face a problem or are engaged in a grand quest.

Consider "Goldilocks and the Three Bears." The setting is a cottage in the woods. The characters are a family of bears and a little girl. The girl faces the problem of finding food and shelter. The bears face two problems. Their porridge is too hot, and a stranger invades their home.

Think of *Hamlet.* You have a setting—the Danish court. You have characters—Hamlet, his mother, his stepfather, his girlfriend. Hamlet has a problem—he must avenge the murder of his father. *Hamlet* is more complicated than "Goldilocks" in certain ways; but, then again, in certain ways it is just as simple.

The first stories that children write are usually pretty muddled. Characters show up and disappear whimsically. Events meander. But when a child understands that stories have a structure, the structure seems like fun, and story writing suddenly makes more sense. The characters are likely to become more interesting and motivated. The plots are likely to have a beginning, when the problem appears, a middle, when the characters deal with the problem, and then an ending, when the characters overcome their problem and begin living happily ever after—or not. The stories may still meander, the characters may still fade in and out. But the story written by a child who has thought about settings, characters, and problems will have at least the rudiments of structure, which is a big improvement over no structure at all.

My favorite game for teaching the fundamentals of story writing is EGG-CARTON TALES. During an EGG-CARTON TALE, your child will make up a story. His story will take place in a specific setting and will feature a predetermined character who must solve a particular problem.

To play, you need two styrofoam egg cartons with the lids still attached. Cut both of the cartons in half and discard one of the halves. You now have three half-cartons.

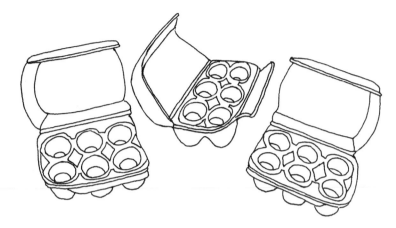

The first carton is called the "setting" carton. Cut six strips of paper small enough to fit inside the individual egg cups. On each strip, write a setting for a story. Here are some suggestions: in a forest, on a pirate ship, in a gangster hideout, at school, in a witch's castle, in a playground, in a toy store, in an amusement park, at the beach, at a horse ranch, in a submarine, in a glue factory.

After you write the strips, set them into the egg carton, one strip per egg cup, and secure each strip with a bit of tape.

The second carton will be your "character" carton. You'll need fascinating characters for this carton. Here are some ideas: a giant, a little girl, an enchanted frog, a witch, a baseball player, a ferocious lion, a TV star, a bank robber, an inventor, a spy, a detective, a pilot, a magician.

Cut six new strips of paper, write a character on each, and tape the strips into the egg cups.

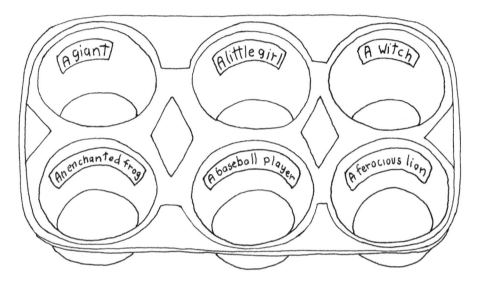

The third carton is the "problem" carton. For this carton, you'll need to select six troubling situations. You can select them from this list if you like: an explosion, overcoming a magic spell, getting lost in the woods, getting caught in a hurricane, having a fight with a bully, hunting for a lost treasure, escaping from a vile villain, getting stuck in quicksand, stopping aliens from invading Earth, getting sick, losing a favorite ring.

Write each problem that you pick on a strip of paper and tape these strips into the egg cups of the third carton. If the words don't fit on the strips, try inventing your own shorthand: for example, *mgc spl* (overcoming a magic spell), and *trsr hnt* (hunting for a lost treasure).

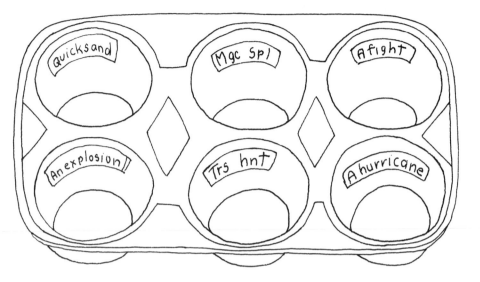

Having prepared all three cartons, you are almost ready for story-telling. Your child will use the egg cartons to discover the setting, character, and problem he must include in his tale. How? First, drop a dime in the "setting" carton, close the carton lid, and hand the carton to your child. Tell him to turn the carton upside down and shake, rattle, and roll the carton. Hold the open end, so the dime won't fall out. After several vigorous shakes, your child should open the carton. The dime will be in one of the egg cups.

Did it land *on a pirate ship*? Then the story must include some on-board scenes. Did it land *in a glue factory*? In that case, the characters may find themselves in sticky situations.

Now transfer the dime to the "character" carton. Your child gives the carton a few shakes, then opens the lid and discovers his story's main character. Finally, slip the dime into the "problem" carton, shake once again, and open the carton to see where the dime has landed. What problem lies under that shaken dime? Is there a magic spell to be exorcized? Is there a monster to be pacified? Whatever it is, your child's main character has to deal with the predicament.

Your child must now tell a story using the egg-carton setting, character, and problem. Children usually find it easiest to start stories by establishing the setting or introducing a character. Some storytellers, though, prefer to state the problem first, and that's just fine. The child can add more characters, include additional settings, or increase the number of problems if such is his whim. There is only one rule: everything that was mandated by the dime and the egg cartons must be addressed before the story ends.

Even if your child is capable of writing his EGG-CARTON TALE, have him tell it out loud instead. First-, second-, and third-graders need opportunities to make up stories without worrying about handwriting, spelling, or slowing their thoughts to a writer's pace. Occasionally they need the freedom to think about plot and only plot. They need chances to let ideas flow without inhibition. They need to tell a few EGG-CARTON TALES—and telling these tales will, in time, help them in their writing, too. For the more they consider the challenge of setting, character, and problem, the more they will master the rudiments of story structure, and when the time comes to write a complete story on paper, which is an immense challenge, the challenge will seem slightly less immense.

If your child likes EGG-CARTON TALES, play it again and again. You will probably want to change the egg-cup strips from time to time. Your child might have some unique ideas for settings, characters, and problems. Go ahead, include them. A few weird ideas that call for improbable plots and bizarre happenings couldn't hurt.

WRITING TO FORM

One of my third-grade students, Lily, wrote stories that were masterpieces of confusion. Her first sentence had nothing to do with her second. Characters appeared and disappeared at random. All was chaos.

Lily wasn't a bad writer. It was just that she, like many other children, didn't realize that stories should have a beginning, a middle, and an end. Nor did she appreciate that events should take place in some sort of logical sequence. As a result, her stories were baffling.

In an effort to help Lily tell a coherent story, I drew up the following form:

GRADES

second and third

MATERIALS

copies of one of the forms on
pages 143–145
two pencils

The Elf's Adventure

Suzie was a _____ elf. She had a _____ and a _____ . Her favorite way to spend the day was _____

_____ .

One day she was _____ at home when in came _____ . Suzie was so happy, she _____

_____ .

Suzie Elf said, "Let's go _____

_____ ."

And so Suzie and _____ went

_____ .

Then three weird things happened. First,
Suzie _____ .
Second, Suzie _____ .
Third, Suzie _____ .
Suzie Elf was so _____ that she

_____ .

"The Elf's Adventure" is a story full of holes. The structural framework is in place—there's a setting and a main character who has an adventure. The sequence is established. The character is introduced in the first part of the story. Then comes the adventure. Afterwards, the main character even has a concluding thought. But the all-important details needed to flesh out a story and make it special are missing. Lily's job was to fill in the blanks.

The Elf's Adventure

Suzie was a ___Silly___ elf. She had a ___bat___ and a ___ball___. Her favorite way to spend the day was ___play baseball___

One day she was ___watching TV___ at home when in came ___her friend___. Suzie was so happy, she ___wiggled her fingers___.

Suzie Elf said, "Let's go ___play baseball in the park___."

And so Suzie and ___her friend___ went ___to the park___.

Then three weird things happened. First, Suzie ___saw a tiger sleeping in the park___. Second, Suzie ___tickled the tiger on his nose___. Third, Suzie ___invited the tiger to play___. Suzie Elf was so ___happy___ that she ___hit a homerun___.

Completing the story wasn't easy for Lily. A couple of times she was confused, unsure about what to write. When this happened, I came to her assistance. I pointed out the elements that she had already put in the story. Since baseball is the elf's favorite way to spend the day, it makes sense for the elf to want to play a game. If there is a tiger in the park, it makes sense to include the tiger in the game. Lily had to follow the structure and pay attention to the sequence imposed by the form. I couldn't spend my whole time helping Lily out, however. I was busy filling in the blanks of my own copy of "The Elf's Adventure."

The Elf's Adventure

Suzie was a ___nasty___ elf. She had a __bat__ and a ___dog___. Her favorite way to spend the day was _tricking all the humans she could_ .

One day she was ___sleeping___ at home when in came _a little boy_. Suzie was so happy, she _began giggling_.

Suzie Elf said, "Let's go _eat lots and lots of ice cream_."

And so Suzie and _her pets and the boy_ went _to an ice cream store_.

Then three weird things happened. First, Suzie _turned all the ice cream into mud_. Second, Suzie _turned the cones into pine cones_. Third, Suzie _turned the fudge sauce into red ants_. Suzie Elf was so ___delighted___ that she _laughed for an hour_.

My story wasn't a bit like Lily's, and this amazed her. She hadn't realized that the same outline could result in two such different adventures—each with a beginning, middle, and end. I assured her that if a thousand different people filled in the form there would be a thousand different stories. Lily was impressed. She wondered how many different ways she herself could fill in the form. Over the next two weeks, Lily and I each wrote two new versions. And that was enough. Just because you can send an elf on 1,000 different adventures doesn't mean you have to do so.

We liked writing fill-in stories, though. So I created new forms. You'll find them at the end of this activity. You can photocopy them or take a few minutes to copy them by hand.

I suggest you work on the first story with your child. Encourage silliness. A funny detail or two never hurts.

The next time you play, pick a new form. You and your child can either work together or you can both compose your own stories and surprise each other with the results. If your ideas overwhelm the blank spaces, feel free to spill over into the margins. As with most of the activities in this book, neatness isn't an issue. You may find it helpful to edit the form by changing a few words here and there.

If your child really loves this game, four forms won't be enough. In that case, make up your own form. It's easier than you'd imagine—if you're willing to borrow from other tales. Think of "Little Red Riding Hood." Start the story. After writing several words, throw in a blank.

A young girl and her _____ lived in the _____. The girl went to visit her _____. On the way she met a wolf. The wolf ran ahead. He wanted to _____ the girl.

You can continue with the tale and let Little Red meet the wolf in Grandma's bed if you want. Or you can make a few changes. You might consider a new ending:

The girl was too _____. She had a trick for the wolf. First she _____. Then she _____. The wolf was so angry, he screamed, "_____." But the girl just _____ and said, "_____ _____."

Fill in the blanks. What have you got? "Little Red Riding Hood" with a difference. And in the difference lies a lesson in story structure.

The Elf's Adventure

Suzie was a _____ elf. She had a _____
and a _____. Her favorite way to spend the day
was _____
_____.

One day she was _____ at home when in
came _____. Suzie was so happy, she _____
_____.

Suzie Elf said, "Let's go _____
_____."

And so Suzie and _____ went
_____.

Then three weird things happened. First,
Suzie _____.
Second, Suzie _____.
Third, Suzie _____.
Suzie Elf was so _____ that she
_____.

One Girl's Adventure

In a _____ town, a _____ girl lived in
a _____ house. One day the girl went for a
_____. While she was _____, she
saw a surprising thing. She saw a _____.
The _____was _____. The girl felt
_____. She wanted to _____,
but she _____ instead.

After a few minutes the _____ said,
"You look _____. Will you _____
with me?"

Here's what happened next: _____

_____

_____

_____.

Friendship

A bear and a mouse were _____. They
_____ together every day. Their favorite game was
_____. They ate together every day. Their favorite
lunch was _____. One day mouse went
to bear's _____. Bear was _____ sad. He
had a problem. Bear was upset because _____.
Mouse wanted to help bear. He tried all sorts of things
to make bear laugh. First he _____.
Then he _____.
Finally he _____.
Nothing worked. Mouse said, "Bear, I want to _____
you with your problem. Tell me what to do."

Bear said, "You can help. You can _____
_____."

Mouse did what bear wanted. Then bear was so
happy he gave mouse a big _____.

An Old Story

In ancient times, a wizard lived in a big _____

_____ .

There was a village nearby and the villagers were

_____ of the wizard. Every morning the wiz-

ard _____ . The villagers were _____

when this happened. Every afternoon the wizard

_____ .

The villagers were _____ when this hap-

pened. Every night the wizard _____ .

The villagers were _____ when this

happened.

Then one day a _____ girl said, "I'm not afraid

of the wizard. I want to be his _____ . I'm going

to visit him today at _____ ."

The villagers were _____ .

The mayor said, "_____

_____ ."

The girl's mother said, "_____

_____ ."

The girl's father said, "_____

_____ ."

But the girl just _____ .

The girl went _____ . She walked

_____ . Finally she _____ .

When she found the wizard, he _____ .

Then a surprising thing happened. The wizard _____

_____ .

The girl _____ .

That's why all the people in the village _____

_____ .

THE THREE-SENTENCE CHALLENGE

GRADES

second and third

MATERIALS

paper
pencil

Becka was a third-grader who loved writing stories. She found it easy to make up characters and weave interesting plots. I was surprised, therefore, to hear her complain bitterly about her most recent homework assignment. Her teacher wanted her to write a short factual report on owls. Becka's class had spent the last several weeks studying the life cycle of owls. She loved learning about these creatures and was proud of the considerable amount of owl lore that she had accumulated. Why, then, did she so resist writing a few paragraphs about her favorite bird?

Becka had learned so much about owls that she was drowning in information. She had no idea how to pick out and summarize the most important facts.

I have found that THE THREE-SENTENCE CHALLENGE is a good game for helping children learn how to summarize information. So I introduced the game to Becka. I showed her this list:

soccer
football
basketball
hockey

I told her to pick one of these four games but not let me know her choice. She should, instead, write three sentences describing the game she had picked. She must not use the name of the game in her description, however. What's more, she couldn't name any of the other games, either; indeed, *all* the words on the list were off limits. When she finished writing, I would read her three sentences. If I could figure out which game she selected, she would get three points. If I couldn't figure it out, she would have to write a fourth sentence. If the fourth sentence gave me enough information to identify the game, she would get two points. If not, she'd have to add yet another sentence. If this sentence did the trick, she would get one point. If not, she would get no points at all in this round of the game.

As Becka noticed immediately, I would have to be honest or the game wouldn't be fair. If I recognized the sport, I had to say so right away. After I promised not to cheat, she wrote the following:

You play with a ball. You throw the ball and kick it. You get points for touchdowns.

It was a reasonable description of football, I thought. I named the sport, congratulated Becka, and awarded her three points. Then I wrote another list and gave it to her to read:

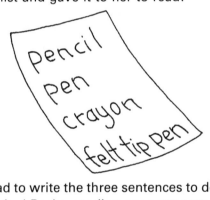

pencil
pen
crayon
felt tip pen

This time, I had to write the three sentences to describe a single item on my list. And Becka, reading my sentences, would have to recognize which object I had described. This is what I wrote:

It is covered with wood. It is usually yellow on the outside. It has an eraser on top.

Becka read the sentences. "It's a pencil," she said. "Can I go again now?"

"Sure," I said. "Here's another list."

"I want a really hard one this time," she said.

Becka wanted a challenge and I delivered one. I wrote a list of these four snacks:

potato chips
corn chips
nacho cheese chips
onion garlic chips

Before she started writing a description of the snack she had picked, I reminded Becka that by the rules of the game, she could not use any of the words on the list. The word *potato*, being on the list, was off limits, even if she wanted to write about potato chips. The word *cheese* was off limits even if she wanted to write about nachos.

Becka moaned, but she didn't concede defeat. After a minute's thought, she wrote:

This is orangy. We had some for snack last week. It has something in it that's in pizza.

That was a fine way to describe nacho cheese chips. I praised Becka for the clever way she had alluded to cheese, the unmentionable, in her description.

"It's your turn now, Peggy," she said. And then she said something else. "We're not really trying to beat the other person, are we? It's not a game against each other. It's just a game for the fun of it."

I agreed, but I could have added one more thought. It's a game for fun, but it also helps children like Becka feel more comfortable picking out and writing the most relevant facts so that any reader can understand her thoughts. There are many things to say about football, but Becka had honed in on the most pertinent information, and in three sentences she had summarized that sport. There are lots of things to say about owls, too. This game helped me explain to Becka that she needed to select the most important and interesting facts in order to complete her homework assignment. THE THREE-SENTENCE CHALLENGE is, in short, a game that teaches a child to sort through and prioritize information, a skill that is central to writing and many other activities.

If you want to play this game at home, all you need are the lists. Each list should have four items. The four should have many things in common. That's what makes it a challenge. Here are a few lists to get you started:

jungle gym seesaw slide swings	sneakers slippers boots loafers
Cinderella Snow White Rapunzel Little Red Riding Hood	car truck bus motorcycle
swimming row boating sailing skiing	lemonade orange juice grapefruit juice apple juice
magazine book newspaper store catalogue	shirt sweater coat dress

I'M A QUIET MOUSE

GRADES

second and third

MATERIALS

a large sheet of paper or oaktag
(at least 18″ × 24″)
colored marker
scissors
twelve index cards
pencil or pen
masking or transparent tape
a large paper clip or old
house key

Ametaphor is a turn of phrase in which, in order to make something more vivid, you link it to something else. You might want to explain, for instance, that Billy was a good swimmer. So you might write: "Billy was a dolphin in water." He wasn't *really* a dolphin, but saying that he was makes you picture the natural ease and lithe gracefulness with which he swam. A few good metaphors will make any piece of writing sparkle. "Beware of false prophets who come to you in sheep's clothing but inwardly are ravenous wolves," the Holy Scriptures say. To write that well is divine.

Adults have no trouble understanding or inventing metaphors, though they may stumble if you ask them to define exactly what a metaphor is. But children are often confused when they confront them. Children have literal minds, and the whole point of metaphoric language is *not* to be literal.

Hillary, a second-grade student, was reading a story about a boy named Ben and was thrown into confusion by a single metaphoric phrase. The author wrote, "Ben was a quiet mouse hiding in the attic." Hillary was dumbfounded. She turned to me and asked, "When did Ben turn into a mouse? I thought he was a boy."

I explained the author's intention. "The sentence that you just read doesn't mean that Ben really is a mouse," I said. "It means he was very quiet. He was as quiet as a mouse. Can you think of a time when you've been that quiet?"

"I'm very quiet in the library," she said.

"As quiet as a mouse?" I asked.

"I guess," she said.

"Then, you're a quiet mouse in the library," I said. "Do you want to know when I'm a quiet mouse?"

"Sure," she answered.

"I'm a quiet mouse when I sleep on the beach. Would you like to know when I'm a grouchy grizzly bear?" I asked.

"Yup," she said.

"I'm a grouchy grizzly bear when I wake up too early in the morning. When are you a grouchy grizzly bear?" I asked.

"When my brother bothers me," she answered without hesitating.

"I know a game we can play that will let me find out when you're a shy turtle, and you'll get to find out when I'm a mean monster. Want to play?" I asked.

I warned her that she would have to spend a few minutes helping me prepare the game materials. But that was all right; she wanted to play. On an 18″ × 24″ sheet of paper, I made an eight-box grid with a colored marker. I placed the board on the floor.

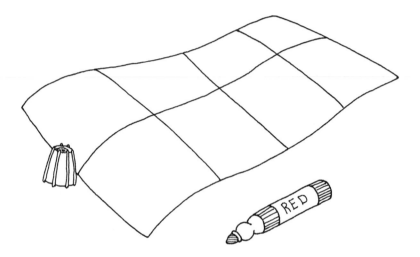

Next I showed Hillary this list of twenty-five unfinished metaphorical sentences:

I'm a quiet mouse when . . .
I'm a grouchy grizzly bear when . . .
I'm a scaredy-cat when . . .
I'm a spooky ghost when . . .
I'm a hungry shark when . . .
I'm a wiggly worm when . . .
I'm a mean witch when . . .
I'm a silly clown when . . .

I'm a nervous rabbit when . . .
I'm a shy turtle when . . .
I'm a kind lamb when . . .
I'm a joyful song when . . .
I'm a clever detective when . . .
I'm a laughing hyena when . . .
I'm a sneaky fox when . . .
I'm a lonely clam when . . .
I'm a noisy thunderstorm when . . .
I'm a cuddly puppy when . . .
I'm a playful kitten when . . .
I'm an angry monster when . . .
I'm a firecracker when . . .
I'm a spoon of honey when . . .
I'm a sneaky fox when . . .
I'm a stubborn mule when . . .
I'm a strong ox when . . .

I told her to select four unfinished sentences and copy them onto index cards, one sentence per card. She shouldn't tell me which ones she had selected, though. It is more fun when the sentences come as a surprise during the game. After she finished, she wrote a large *H* (for Hillary) on the back of each card.

Meanwhile, I took four index cards for myself. I picked my own sentence fragments and copied them onto the cards, one sentence per card. On the back of each card I wrote a large *P* (for Peggy).

Next we took turns taping the cards on the game board. We put one card in each section of the game board, making sure the *P*'s and *H*'s were face up.

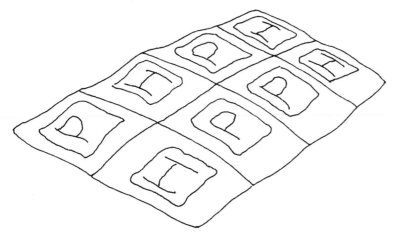

Finally we needed a token to toss onto the game board. We used a paper clip, but any old thing would do, a house key, a quarter, a pinched-off corner of a sponge, so long as it won't roll around too much.

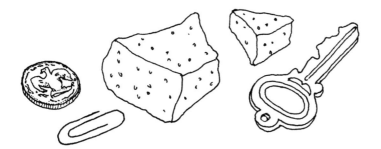

Our preparations complete, we were ready to play. The goal of this game is to collect all four of your opponent's cards. You do this by tossing the token. If you have good aim, the token will land on one of your opponent's cards. Then you turn over the card, read the sentence fragment, and try to complete the sentence in a reasonable way. If you can do this, you win the card.

When Hillary understood the object of the game, we took our places standing side by side about two feet away from the board, which was on the floor. I took the first turn. I threw the paper clip and hoped it would land on a box containing an *H* card. It did. I took off the taped card and read "I am a hungry shark when . . ." I wanted to keep this card, and there was only one way for me to do so. I had to find sensible words to finish the sentence. I stared at the unfinished sentence; I stared at the ceiling. I stared at Hillary. Finally I said, "I am a hungry shark when I miss my dinner."

That make sense. It was plausible. As a result, I got to keep the card. Now it was Hillary's turn. She threw the clip. Her aim was good. She landed on a *P* card, lifted it off the board, and read, "I'm a scaredy-cat when . . ." Hillary had no trouble finishing the sentence. "I'm a scaredy-cat when I hear noises in the dark." That made perfect sense. Hillary won her first card. If she hadn't made sense, I would have coached her until she arrived at a better sentence. Similarly, if she hadn't liked my sentence about being a shark when I miss dinner, I would have had to keep looking for a way to complete the sentence that did make sense to her and me both.

Then it was my turn next. I tossed the paper clip, and it landed on a *P* card. You can't collect your own cards in this game. So, reluctantly I turned the clip over to Hillary. She was so excited by the chance to pull ahead of me that she missed the board completely. When you miss the board you also miss a chance to capture a card. It was my turn again. We kept tossing the paper clip until Hillary won the game by collecting all four *P* cards.

I can't deny that I helped her to win by tossing the clip in the wrong direction once or twice. But that was my secret; she didn't have to know. And it was my secret that, by playing this game, Hillary was accustoming herself to one of the most difficult figures of speech for children to learn: the metaphor.

PART FIVE
MADE WITH PRIDE

The activities in this section will take you more time to complete than the other activities in this book. Length is part of their purpose. When children sit down to write, they often begin with enthusiasm, but after a few words make it onto the page, the enthusiasm wanes and the child is ready to quit. That can be a serious problem. Children can't develop as writers if they only write a few words now and a few words later. Good writing requires sustained effort.

The eight projects in this section are designed to strengthen a child's ability to make a such an effort. SHAPE BOOKS describes how you can create books that look like cats, baseball caps, and puppies. A cat-shaped book is an odd idea, certainly. Sometimes, though, a weirdly shaped book can build a young child's enthusiasm for writing.

Perhaps your child would prefer composing an alphabet book. In this section you will discover how to write a special one—a very, very ANGRY ALPHABET BOOK. The twenty-six pages may take a dozen days to finish. That's okay. Moving from *A* to *Z*, your child will experience the pleasing sensation of seeing his words cover page after page.

THE LONGEST STORY EVER WRITTEN offers you and your child an unusual and almost foolproof way to write an immensely long story.

You will also find instructions for writing your own plays, producing homemade comics, and creating personalized board games.

These activities all demand an extra effort, commitment of time, concentration, and intellectual stamina. A child who successfully follows through on such a project can look back and say with pride "I did that. It's special. It was hard to finish, but that didn't stop me."

Of course, you don't need to complete a project in a single sitting. Spread the work out. Spend half an hour or so on Tuesday and finish a comic-book page. Then resume work on Sunday. If you finish two pages a week, you will have created an eight-page production in a month's time. Although some of the activities are unusual, you won't have to purchase elaborate equipment. Paper, pencil, oaktag and a few other household items are all you'll need.

You might consider starting one of these projects during school vacation. Your child will be hanging around the house, and you will have a good motive for finding some way to occupy his time. Why not help him write a play or create a board game? In doing so, you give your child the experience of making a sustained effort with pencils and paper. You will also create family memories. Long after the vacation ends, your child will recall your time together and the shared fun of writing.

SHAPE BOOKS

GRADES

first, second, and third

MATERIALS

blank paper
construction paper
pencil
stapler
scissors
colored pencils or crayons

*B*ooks are usually rectangular in shape, which makes them easy to put away on shelves but dull to look at. Why not change their shape now and then? It's amazing how a child's interest in books and writing will sometimes perk up simply because a book comes in some other shape, maybe a very unusual shape.

That was the case with Blanche, a second-grader who loved to draw and tell stories but hated to write. When she did sit down to write, under the pressure of her teachers, she was so stingy with verbal expression that the stories she produced never went beyond three or four words. She wrote a story about her new bicycle that read, in its entirety, "It is nice." She wrote a story about Halloween that began, "It is fun"—and went no further. Blanche was not proud of these stories, but she wouldn't or couldn't put more effort into them. She found writing too painful.

She did love to draw, however, and because she had three kittens at home, as she explained, she got lots of practice drawing cats. This led me to wonder if, by making use of her interest in cats, she could be encouraged to extend herself a little more in her efforts to write. I assigned her to write a story about cats, a story that would begin with a drawing. She liked that part of the assignment and carefully sketched a wonderful picture. With my prodding, she added a sentence to the page:

Cats are silly

It was another three-word story, but I deemed it a good start. For the first time she seemed proud of her work. That was promising. To build on this success, I suggested we make an entire cat book: not just a book about cats, but a book that literally looked like a cat.

To create this unusual book, I took a blank sheet of paper and drew on it the outline of a seated cat:

On pages 164–165, you can find a model of this same cat, along with some other SHAPE BOOK models, in case you want to make your own cat-shaped book.

Next I made a pile of five sheets of blank paper and two sheets of red construction paper. I put the cat drawing on top of this pile, and carefully—very carefully—used the scissors to cut along the outline of the cat. Now I had six white cats and two red ones.

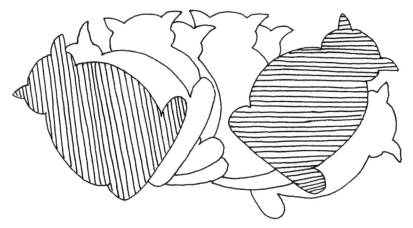

The white sheets were for the innards of the book. The red sheets were for the front and back covers.

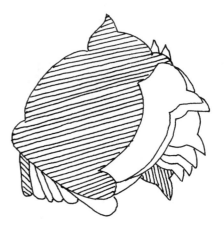

With the papers in the right places, I tacked a row of staples along the left-hand side of the cat. Then I drew some feline details on the front cover.

It was cat-shaped, and it was a book. Best of all, Blanche expressed guarded interest in writing something special in this uniquely shaped volume.

"I bet you have lots of funny stories about your kittens," I said. "Why not write a few in your book? You could tell about one bit of cat mischief on each page. You could start each page with a drawing and then add words."

Blanche liked this plan and went to work on page one. As I expected, she drew the picture without hesitation. Words had to come next. But what if writing proved too tedious? Would Blanche sour on the project? She chewed her pencil. I was nervous myself.

She said, "I want to write, 'My cats like to jump. They look like frogs.' But I don't think I can."

For Blanche, that was, indeed, an ambitious writing plan. She needed reassurance that all would be well if she made the effort.

"I'm sure you can do it," I said. "Just go one word at a time. I'll help, if you need it."

Blanche plunged into writing. The first two words, "My cats," came easily. But she didn't know how to spell *like*, and this upset her. I wrote *like* on a piece of scrap paper and gave it to her to copy. She smiled and continued writing. She managed to write *to* and *jump* on her own and then proceeded steadily into the sentence about frogs.

By now she was very tired and wanted to stop for the day. We both observed that it might take several weeks to complete the book.

It did take a while to finish. But over those weeks, Blanche learned to write without worrying. She fretted less about spelling.

In fact, she was willing to tackle a few unknown words on her own. She discovered that I could read her stories even if there were spelling and handwriting errors. Her proud mother could read the stories, too, and so could her delighted father. Blanche hadn't totally overcome her unease about writing, but she had made a start.

Blanche loved her cat book, but cats may not suit your child. In that case, you should pick a different shape. Some shapes work best when the staples that bind the book are on the left; other shapes work best if the staples are on the top, so that the book opens like a notebook pad. Here are some ideas for possible books. I've drawn lines indicating the staples so you can see how the books open and close.

A cat book:

A house book:

A fish book:

A snake book:

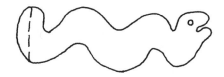

A diamond book:

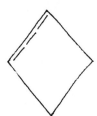

A baseball cap book:

164

A puppy book:

A guitar book:

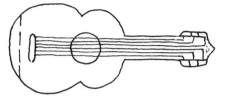

An ice cream book:

A basketball book:

Don't be afraid to draw a SHAPE BOOK. I've found that children are very tolerant of oddly formed guitars or puppies, so your original drawings don't have to be very good. Indeed, even primitive cut-outs delight most children. And once they are fascinated by the cover of the book and its shape, it is an easy thing to get them to pick up a pencil and write a few words, and then a few words more, in a volume that looks infinitely more appealing than the old dull rectangle of ordinary books.

ANGRY ALPHABET BOOK

GRADES

first and second

MATERIALS

blank paper
construction paper or
posterboard
pencils
crayons or colored pencils
hole puncher
loose-leaf rings

When children sit down to write, they should have the opportunity to express happy thoughts and carefree humor, but also other kinds of sentiments, even angry and outrageous ones. Anger is, after all, a true enough emotion, and it ought to have its place in what children write. That is the function of ANGRY ALPHABET BOOK. Writing an ANGRY ALPHABET BOOK allows, even encourages, children to compose all kinds of ferocious and hostile statements. Naturally, when you sit down with your own child to compose such statements, you may want to establish some sensible limits. The purpose of an ANGRY ALPHABET BOOK is not to allow a child to vent his knowledge of playground curse words. Even anger has its decorum. But an angry book does give a child the chance to engage in a bit of zesty mischief and playful nastiness—and thereby deepen his experience of putting words on paper.

On the first page of an ordinary alphabet book, the author explains that "A is for apple" and the illustrator paints a shiny red apple. The next page says "B is for ball" and shows you the well-painted bounce of a ball. An ANGRY ALPHABET BOOK follows the same procedure, with text and illustration moving along letter by letter. But every page in an ANGRY ALPHABET BOOK expresses outrage and anger—blended (and this is also the point) with a bit of humor. You and your child must think of the alphabetic statements yourselves. You might start, for instance, with *A is for angry Andrew.* Andrew, I hope you'll agree, will be fun to draw.

What about B? I like *B is for a bumpy, bratty, bad-breath bug—* though any statement you choose will be just as good, so long as all of the important words begin with *b*.

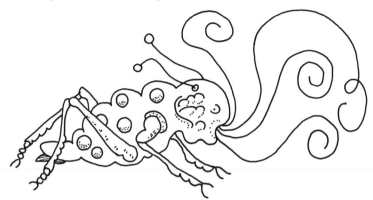

C might be *C is for crazy, creepy, Cabbagehead.*

You continue through the alphabet, filling each page with an acerbic allotment of alliterations and maybe a few nonalliterative words if need be. Some of the letters may give your child a bit of trouble when it comes to thinking of angry words, and if that happens you may want to sit down with the child and thumb through a children's dictionary (an adult dictionary will be too difficult for children to dip into). Skimming through *D*, for instance, I find *destructive*, *disgusting*, *dirty*, and *drooling*, each one of which opens a vast region of alphabetic possibilities. Letters such as *X* or *Z* may be tougher, but the dictionary will never let you down.

A few imaginative stretches—a *zooney* or two, for instance—may be necessary and should always be welcomed.

It will take time to write this book. You can speed the process by writing some of the pages yourself, though there's really no need to rush. An ANGRY ALPHABET BOOK should be written at a relaxed and thoughtful pace, the better to savor and enjoy.

When you do complete the pages, you'll want to bind the book. I suggest using a hoop binding method. A couple of sturdy sheets of paper, perhaps construction paper or posterboard, can serve as the front and back covers.

Next, punch three holes along the left-hand side of your papers and join the sheets with three loose-leaf rings. You can get the rings in any stationery store.

If the ANGRY ALPHABET BOOK is a success, you may want to start a new book. Consider writing *The Horror Alphabet Book, The Silly, Foolish Alphabet Book, A Doll's Alphabet Book, A Baseball Alphabet Book,* or *The Completely Disgusting Alphabet Book.*

WRITE A LETTER

GRADES

first, second, and third

MATERIALS

stationery
pencil
postage stamps

*B*urt was outraged. He had just learned that from now on his branch of the public library would be closed on Saturdays. "It's not fair," he said. "Saturday is the best day to go!"

I sympathized. And I suggested that he write a letter to the mayor, complaining about the closing.

"Will he open the library?" Burt asked.

"Probably not right away, but if he gets lots of letters about this he'll know that people are unhappy. If enough people are unhappy, he may come up with a way to open the library again. Anyway, he may write you back and explain why the library had to be closed. I can't promise, but he might."

"I'll do it," Burt said.

I took out a piece of paper and Burt got down to work. He wanted the letter to be perfect, and so I promised to help him spell any hard words. He wrote in pencil, which made it easy to correct any mistakes. After he finished, we put the letter in an envelope, addressed it, stamped it, and took it to the mailbox.

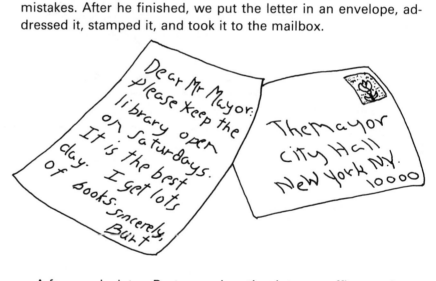

A few weeks later, Burt came bursting into my office waving a letter from the mayor. It was a form letter, but Burt didn't care. It was his own letter, addressed to him from the mayor. Not even his father got mail from the mayor! Burt decided he wanted to write another letter—this time to the president of the United States.

It's quite easy to arrange for your mailbox to be stuffed with letters addressed to your child. Just because he doesn't vote (yet) doesn't mean that he can't write to his elected representatives. Here is the president's address:

> The White House
> 1600 Pennsylvania Avenue
> Washington, D.C. 20500

Write senators and members of Congress, too. For them use this address:

> United States Congress
> Washington, D.C. 20510

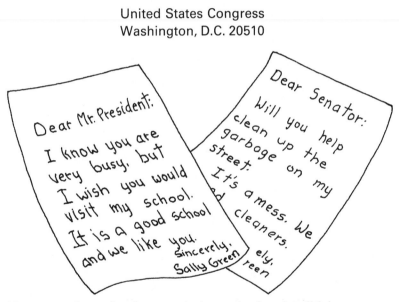

Dear Mr. President:
I know you are very busy, but I wish you would visit my school. It is a good school and we like you.
Sincerely,
Sally Green

Dear Senator:
Will you help clean up the garbage on my street? It's a mess. We ... cleaners.
...ely,
...reen

Use your phone book to track down the local politicians.

What if your child doesn't feel like writing to politicians? Don't put away the stationery yet. Your child might enjoy writing the author of his favorite book or the leading batter of his favorite baseball team.

How does your child send these letters? How will he find the right addresses? With your help, he can obtain a wonderful publication called *The Kid's Address Book*, written by Michael Levine and published by Perigee Books. Mr. Levine has compiled 186 pages of addresses that will help your child get in touch with an amazing array of people.

Yet even without this book, and without much effort, either, you can find nearly any address you want. If your child is moved to correspond with an author, for instance, simply address a letter in care of the writer's publisher.

Write to athletes in care of their teams.

Here's another idea: send letters to food companies. Has your child started eating a new cereal? Is it as great as the ads promise? Your child can write to the company and tell them so. Is the cereal absolutely revolting? Let your child write to the company and complain.

Has your child purchased a new game lately? A toy or a doll? Why not have the child write to the company that made the product and tell them about it? Maybe the doll is the finest your child ever owned; maybe it's cheap and badly made; maybe the clothes rip the minute you try to put them on. Whatever the case, your child can tell all in a carefully composed letter.

Dear Health Buds:
Your cereal is awful. I hate the chocolate covered nuts. It is loaded with fat and sugar. How can it be healthy?
Sincerely,
Zach Rubin

Will your child really want to write these letters? Under the right circumstances, even first-graders are eager to send thoughts, opinions, and compliments through the mail. What are the right circumstances? Give your child lots of help and support. It's okay to take dictation, for instance. Your child says the words and you write them down. The child signs, the adult sends. As a next step, let your child dictate the letter to you first, and then have him copy it in his own hand. You can explain that people are more inclined to answer a letter when they see that a child has bothered to write it himself. Inspired by such a possibility, your child might want to write the letter on his own from scratch. You can certainly give spelling help on demand. You can also offer to correct any mistakes in the final copy. Writing in pencil or erasable pen makes this job easy.

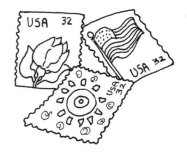

If you smooth the way, your child may become an avid letter writer, quick to send off his thoughts whenever the occasion arises. You'd better stock up on stamps, just in case.

BOARD GAMES

GRADES

first, second, and third

MATERIALS

drawing paper or posterboard
pencil
one playing die
paper money (homemade or
store bought)
game tokens
colored pencils or crayons

Monopoly, which is based on finance and real estate, is a very exciting board game to play. But David and I came up with a game that, in our opinion, was more exciting. Our game was based on witchcraft, which is even scarier than finance and real estate. We called the game Witchville.

The board looked something like a Monopoly board. It was a road divided into many segments.

We didn't fill our board with Atlantic City real estate holdings, though. Instead, our game took place in the imaginary town of Witchville, a village populated by wizards, ghouls, ghosts, and, of course, witches. You don't wheel and deal real estate in Witchville, though you do get richer or poorer depending on where you land on the board.

If you're lucky, you'll hit one of these spots:

If you're unlucky, you'll land on one of these:

Of course, we also had a space labeled GO.

We began the game with $1,000 each in play money. We both had game tokens—a safety pin for me and a paper clip for David. We placed our tokens on GO and took turns rolling a single die and moving our tokens around the board. Every time we landed on a square, we either gained money or lost. If we got richer, we took money from a money pile. If we got poorer, we put money back into the pile. We timed our play, and after half an hour, we counted our loot. The richest player won. If one player went into financial bankruptcy before the half-hour time limit, the game ended early and the solvent player declared victory.

Sound simple? Yes—except that with Witchville the real work, the main activity from a writing point of view, was the making of the board.

We started with a sheet of drawing paper that was 18″ × 24″. After dividing the board into sixteen spaces, we needed to write instructions in each space. We did all our writing in pencil. That way it was easy to make changes or corrections. We illustrated some of the spaces with colored pencils.

David and I worked on the board for many weeks, devoting fifteen to twenty minutes of every tutoring session to filling in new spaces. We helped each other come up with ideas. We shared the writing and the drawing. We tried to include an equal number of win-money and lose-money spaces. We decided that the most you could win on any space was $100 and the most you could lose was $40.

Halfway through our first game, though, we realized that we were both getting too rich too fast. We had to make some changes.

I changed a "win" space to a "lose" spot:

David changed a space, too:

After a little more fiddling, we started up the game again. Our adjustments worked. We spent the next half-hour on an exciting, often frustrating, financial roller-coaster ride.

It's entirely possible to make other games, too. With a student named John, I once made a game with a jungle theme. We lost money in sinister quicksand traps and we became rich by stumbling into caves filled with hidden treasure.

With a student named Dori, I made a game with a city theme. Each space had the name of a spot in New York City. If we landed in Central Park, we gained money. If we landed at the F.A.O. Schwarz toy store, money disappeared.

Your child might prefer a farm game (feed a baby lamb and you win cash; break eggs and you lose), a rocket-ship game (invent a super fuel and you win money; float out in space without a lifeline and you lose), or a detective game (catch crooks and get the dough; miss an important clue and you're busted).

Before starting such a game, you do, of course, need play money. There are three ways to get your hands on fake dollars. You can borrow them from a Monopoly set or from some other game. You can buy play money in a toy store. Or you can spend about fifteen minutes making your own currency. For one-dollar bills, cut a few sheets of yellow construction paper down to dollar-bill size. Then make ten-dollar bills from blue construction paper and one-hundred-dollar bills from red paper. About thirty one-dollar bills, eighty ten-dollar bills, and thirty hundred-dollar bills should do. You will also need a playing die.

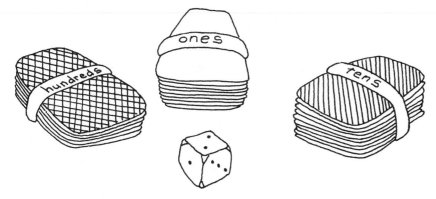

If your child enjoyed making and playing his first board game, you might make a second or a third, or even a whole collection. Did the Parker Brothers get started this way? Did Milton or Bradley? Maybe they did.

FAMILY JOURNAL

GRADES

first, second, and third

MATERIALS

notebook
pencil

How was your week? What was the best thing that happened? What was the worst? Did your child have a good week? Did anything unusual happen? A FAMILY JOURNAL is a collective diary in which you and everyone else in the family writes down responses to questions like these.

All you need is a notebook filled with paper. Make a title page on the first sheet of the notebook:

Put the week's date at the top of the second sheet:

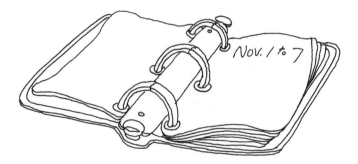

When you have the chance, gather your family together so that each person can write an entry. Each person records the best or worst thing that happened during the week. One sentence will do.

A child who is too young to write can dictate his contribution, and should anyone feel like illustrating an entry, hand over the crayons. Then close the journal until next week.

Don't be too exacting or formal in your journal keeping. You might decide to make Saturday the day for gathering everyone to write the entries; but if one week you pull out the journal on Friday instead, that won't be too terrible. You might write down your wishes instead of recording actual events. What happens if one family member is away and can't share in journal writing? Don't worry; there's always next week. If someone drops out of journal writing for a week or so, that's okay, too. Just try to contribute something to the notebook on a fairly regular basis. Then, at the end of a month or six weeks, when you and your child (or children) sit together and flip back through the pages, you'll chuckle. You'll moan. You'll sigh. You'll remember.

Some families may not take to journal writing. They may find that keeping a journal is too much trouble, or that it requires a weekly schedule more orderly than can be arranged. But for the families who do enjoy keeping a journal, the moment when everyone sits down to record entries can be a valuable time in the education of a child. There is nothing better than a FAMILY JOURNAL for making a child feel that writing words on paper is part of life and love, not just an irksome task imposed by the faraway authorities of that distant institution, the school.

COMIC BOOKS

GRADES

second and third

MATERIALS

unlined paper
pencil
crayons or colored pencils
plastic folder
stapler

*P*arents sometimes try to discourage children from reading comics, but not necessarily for any good reason. If a child reads with enthusiasm, that is a wonderful thing, and if the reading matter consists of comic books, why complain? Even a lowly comic book can serve as a stepping stone to a more serious interest in reading and writing.

One way to make an interest in comic books more productive is to go about drafting your own comic-book adventures. That is what I did with Max, who was, at the age of eight, something of an expert on comic-book superheroes. Max loved the *pows, zings,* and *bangs.* He appreciated the characters' superhuman powers. He understood comic-book dialogue.

What's more, Max was an artist who specialized in airplanes, rockets, laser guns, and military tanks. Considering all this, I was sure that, given the opportunity, Max could produce a fabulous action comic. I proposed the project, and he was unconditionally enthusiastic.

Superhero comic-book writers need extraordinary characters to populate their stories. So our first task was to invent such characters. Max had a fine idea. He wanted to include a Martian mouse who would be endowed with astonishing powers. I suggested a second leading character: a superdog defender of planet Earth.

Next decision: Should our two characters be friends or enemies? Max thought enemies would offer more plot possibilities, and I agreed. Our heroes would be mortal foes. How should the story begin? Again, Max had a good plan. He proposed that the evil-minded Supermouse should travel from Mars to Earth—with wicked plans of conquest.

We had to design the first page. Comic books have a special look. Each page is divided into a number of frames of different shapes and sizes.

I wanted the frames of our first sheet to be especially interesting. I took a piece of unlined paper and designed it like this:

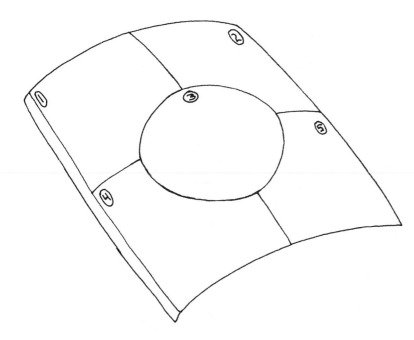

I left a half-inch margin on the lefthand side so that later it would be easy to bind our book. I told Max that each frame in a comic-book story included three components: the drawing, the dialogue bubbles, and the narration. *Narration* was a new word for Max, but when I explained that narration is the writing at the top or bottom of the frame, he understood immediately.

We agreed that for each frame we would write the narration first. Then we could draw pictures and add dialogue bubbles. Up until now, I was in firm control of this project, but I wasn't sure how to begin the story. So Max took over. For our first frame, he announced, we would show Supermouse on Mars stuffing ammunition into a suitcase as he prepares for his trip to Earth. Max wrote the narration on top. I drew the mouse and wrote words in a bubble.

For the next frame, we changed roles. This time I had the story idea. I wrote the narration and also drew the mouse. Max drew extra characters in the background of the frame and filled in the bubbles.

I didn't aim for precision drawing. I've found that most children don't mind stick figures, oddly drawn animals, peculiar buildings, or bizarre trees.

In this way, going frame by frame, we finished the first page in about twenty minutes.

During Max's next appointment, we tackled page two. It also took us about twenty minutes, although it only had three frames.

We worked on the comic for several weeks. After a galaxy-shattering battle, the two superheroes became good friends. Operating together, they defeated common enemies across the universe. Rocket ships and armored flying tanks whirled around the Milky Way. Titanic explosions shook nearly every page. Our comic book demanded all of Max's talents as a military artist.

The pages looked quite good, but, lacking color, not good enough. A comic without color is a sad sight. I took a box of crayons from a drawer and we set about illuminating our manuscript. We made a stunning cover page.

Finally, we put the whole book inside a see-through plastic folder, the kind that comes with a plastic rib. We stapled the folder and book together. Then we slipped the plastic rib over the staples. The finished comic book looked swell.

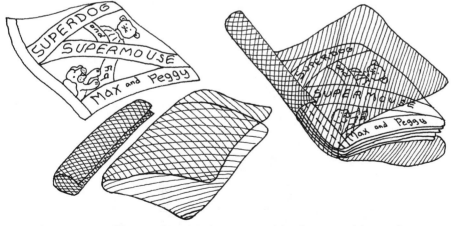

If you are willing to spend the necessary time on this project, you can make comics at your house, too. Start with a story idea.

Imagine a character or two. In my experience, children have an easy time coming up with plots and characters, but if you or your child get stuck, here's a list to trigger your imaginations.

CHARACTERS	PLOT POSSIBILITIES
• a mad scientist • his robot • a policewoman • her talking dog	The scientist, aided by his robot, steals the world's biggest diamond. A brilliant policewoman and her talking dog capture the thief.
• a third-grade boy • his younger sister • a friendly ghost • a school bully	A third-grader has a problem. The school bully is picking on his little sister. He meets a friendly ghost who haunts his school. Together they outsmart the bully.
• an inventor • her cat • her dog	An inventor invents a time machine. She enters with her cat and dog. She goes back to the time of dinosaurs. She has to rescue her dog from a Tyrannosaurus rex.

TIME NOW 1995 AD   GO TO 100,000 BC

Once you have a plot in mind, design your first page in an interesting way.

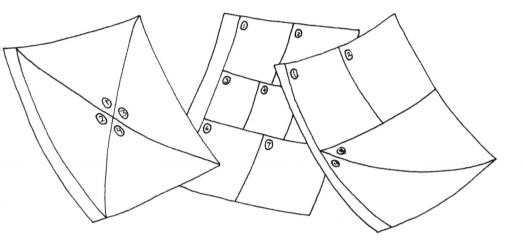

Now begin the first frame. As Edward Gibbon said about writing *The Decline and Fall of the Roman Empire*, after the first sentence, the rest comes easily. When you and your child finish your first comic book, you may well decide to write a sequel or two. True, your child may start walking around the house mumbling, *"Pow,"* *"Zing,"* and *"Bang."* But since a child's literary career is at stake, may I suggest you zing along?

PLAYS AND PLAYERS

GRADES

second and third

MATERIALS

paper
pencil
plastic folder
stapler
optional: toy figures, props,
costumes

*R*yan didn't mind writing a sentence or two. But if she had to write more than that, she balked. In first grade, writing a single-sentence story is a fine accomplishment. "I made a chocolate cake with my mommy" is an excellent story for a six- or seven-year-old. By second grade the same story is only moderately impressive. A third-grader who can't write more than a couple of sentences has a problem. Ryan was in third grade. She had a problem.

Usually, when children have trouble writing, they also have a problem with reading, but that was not Ryan's situation. She could and did read books that would challenge the average sixth-grader. She loved to read. She also loved to tell stories. If you took up a pencil and let Ryan dictate her ideas, she would happily prattle on while you filled page after page with her words.

Why, then, did Ryan find it so hard to write her own stories? First, she didn't feel comfortable with the physical work involved in writing. By third grade, most children print letters without thinking. The strokes are automatic. Not so with Ryan. She had to think about each letter, which meant that writing required vast amounts of concentration. She was a poor speller, too. She had to sound out almost every word she wrote, which was horribly tedious.

The combination of poor handwriting and spelling meant that Ryan spent almost as much time on two sentences as other children spend on two paragraphs. By the time she finished writing her couple of sentences, she was exhausted.

This led to another problem. Ryan saw her classmates turning out stories two and three pages long. Some kids wrote even longer tales. Ryan compared these stories with her own meager compositions and was mortified. Writing was a source of misery for her, never of pride or pleasure.

What Ryan needed was to write something really long—something she could feel proud to have composed, yet something that wouldn't overtax her skills. But what sort of writing assignment comes in two-sentence snippets and still manages to be long?

An answer presented itself one day when Ryan told me about her favorite book. It was a fantasy tale about a magic kingdom in fairyland.

"It's the best book ever written," she declared as she began telling me the story.

Actually, she didn't so much tell the story as act it out. She became every character in the book. She gestured, jumped up and down, bounced around the room. It was quite a show. And it gave me an idea.

"Ryan, would you like to write a play about a fairy kingdom?" I said.

Ryan nodded her approval and then asked, "But how do you write a play?"

"First we need an idea for a good story. We could have—"

Ryan interrupted me: "I want good fairies and bad fairies who fight each other. The good fairies have a magic crown and the bad fairies want to capture it."

Ryan appropriated this idea from "the best book ever written." That was all right with me. When you borrow ideas, borrow from the masters.

"Now we need characters," I said. "Your book has a lot of people. That's good for a book, but hard for a play. I think we had better start with four characters—two for you and two for me. I'll write the lines for my two people and you'll write the lines for yours," I said.

After a brief discussion, we came up with four interesting personalities: Big Nasty, queen of the evil fairies; Little Nasty, Big Nasty's assistant; Lovely, queen of the good fairies; and Kindness, a gentle, good-hearted wizard.

Ryan wanted the part of Lovely and agreed to take on Little Nasty. I was happy enough with my lot: Big Nasty and Kindness.

"I do believe we're ready to write the first scene," I said. "Where should it take place?" Ryan had no idea, so I continued making proposals. "We could start in Big Nasty's throne room. Big Nasty could be making plans to steal the magic crown."

I took a sheet of notebook paper and wrote:

Scene One-- In Big Nasty's throne room. Big Nasty and Little Nasty are talking.

"I know how to begin," I said. "Can I write first?"
Ryan nodded a grateful yes. I wrote Big Nasty's first line.

Big Nasty: I must have Lovely's crown. I must have it no matter what.

After writing, I explained why I put Big Nasty's name and a colon first before the actual words. Ryan understood this right away. She had read some plays in school. Next, I said my lines aloud, with as much theatrical tone as I could manage. Ryan realized that her character, Little Nasty, must respond to Big Nasty's pronouncement. She had an idea and put it down on the paper. (I've put the correct spelling above Ryan's less than accurate versions.)

Little Nasty: Kindness (guards) gards the (crown) croun.

I added a new line:

Big Nasty: My magic is stronger than his. I just need the right spell. Get my spellbook.

Ryan took up her pencil:

Little Nasty: (Here) Her your (majesty) Magste.

192

I added:

Big Nasty: I could turn Kindness into
a toad.

Ryan continued:

Little Nasty: He (likes) (being) toad)
licks beeing a
to de.

Without a word of complaint, Ryan had written three sentences. It's true, she had misspelled seven words, but I didn't care about that. She felt tired, though, and needed a break. So we stopped writing for a few minutes, but we didn't abandon the play. We acted out the dialogue as written so far. I sat in a chair and adopted a regal air. Ryan stood by my side. We read our lines. Then we discussed what should happen next. Refreshed and inspired by our reading and talk, we started writing again.

Big Nasty: Here's a good spell. It will put
Kindness to sleep for 100 years.

Little Nasty: Good, good, make the spell.

Big Nasty : I need magic brew. Get my
cauldron and magic powders.

Little Nasty: OK.

Once again, we stopped writing and read our lines—starting from the beginning. We were pleased with the action so far. We both agreed, though, that this was enough for one day. As Ryan dropped our two finished sheets of paper into a folder, she smiled and said, "I bet this play will be TEN PAGES!"

"It might be, by the time we're done," I said. "You know, it will take us several weeks to finish. Maybe we can act it out for your parents when it's completely written."

Ryan thought this was a fine idea. The upcoming performance gave her purpose. After we finished the first scene—making a magic spell—we went on to scene two. Scene two took place in Queen Lovely's castle. It starred the good queen and the wizard.

Initially, I came up with most of the ideas. My contributions moved the action along. As we continued writing, however, Ryan began participating more equally. In fact, by the final scene she was contributing some of the best thoughts. Eventually she insisted on adding extra characters so that the story could get a bit more complex.

It took six weeks to finish writing and another two weeks to prepare the performance. The play was a great success—both dramatically and academically. Ryan and I had been working together for just ten weeks and her writing was already undergoing a transformation.

Playwriting was so successful with Ryan that I decided to try it out with another student—Roy. Roy collected little figures. He had toy soldiers, cowboys, and tiny monsters jammed into a shoe box. Roy liked the idea of writing a play, but he wanted his toy figures to perform the action. We wrote a play about good soldiers in a war with bad monsters. As we set down each bit of dialogue, we used his figures as puppets.

The figures roamed about my work table while we gave them voices. As the plot developed, we built tissue-box mountains and paper-bag caves to meet the demands of our story. We had a grand time reading lines aloud and moving the figures. Each time we worked together we would act out the story to date and then add a few more lines. At the end of several weeks, we had a first-rate play.

If you want to write plays with your child, you might like a few scenarios to help you get started. Here's a chart of plots, characters, and scenes you can use, if you want. You can, of course, switch ideas around or make any other adjustments you desire.

CHARACTERS	PLOT	POSSIBLE SCENES
• two best friends • an elf • a giant	Two friends discover a castle filled with treasure. But to get the treasure the friends must rescue an elf from a wicked giant.	1. Finding the castle and the treasure. 2. Saving the elf.
• a courageous knight • a brave princess • an evil wizard • a fearsome dragon	An evil wizard and his mean dragon try to take over the kingdom.	1. The dragon is about to attack the castle. 2. Fighting the dragon in the wizard's cave.
• a scientist • the scientist's friend (later a lion) • a bank robber	A scientist invents a formula that can change a person into an animal. To change back, you must take a second dose of the formula. A friend of the scientist agrees to test the formula. He turns into a lion.	1. The formula is ready. The scientist's friend takes a drink and becomes a lion. 2. There is a bank next to the lab. A robbery is in progress. The lion saves the day.

Naturally it is a good idea to bind these plays into a book once you have finished writing. You can follow the same procedure as in COMIC BOOKS. While the writing itself gives children experience, the sight of their own finished dramas, bound and perhaps even illustrated, gives them pride.

THE LONGEST STORY EVER WRITTEN

GRADES

first, second, and third

MATERIALS

adding-machine tape
pencil
paper
optional: ruler

What's the longest story ever written? *The Guinness Book of Records* names something called *Les Hommes de Bonne Volonté* by Louis-Henri Farigoule, whoever he was, as the world's longest story. It goes on for twenty-seven volumes. Still, I'll bet that one of my young students, Anna, wrote the longest story ever written by a child—if length can be measured in feet and inches, and not in the number of pages and volumes. This longest of all stories was called "The Adventures of Tom Turtle."

Anna didn't even like to write, so how did she manage to produce a story that could compete with a Guinness record breaker? By using adding-machine tape. There you have it—the secret to a long, long, long story. Anna wrote her masterpiece on a roll of adding-machine tape.

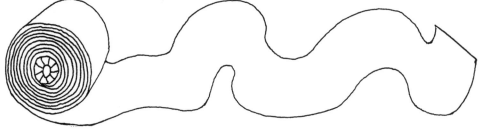

Word by word, the story got longer and longer. By the time Anna had recorded the first dozen words, her narrative was over a foot long.

By the time she had written about the turtle's trip to an underwater kingdom, the story stretched across my workroom. By the time she had described the turtle's escape from a giant octopus, the story spanned four flights of stairs from my tutoring office to the first-floor landing.

It took several weeks to finish the tale. In general, Anna spent just ten to fifteen minutes during our tutoring sessions adding words to her story. When we finished writing for the day, she measured the tape. When her father came to pick her up, she insisted on unfurling the whole thing to show off her latest additions.

As the tape stretched farther and farther, Anna's pleasure in writing grew, too. One day, she asked to write for our entire hour.

"Anna, do you really want to write for a whole hour?" I asked incredulously.

"Yes," she answered. "Writing is my favorite thing."

Why did she say that? Writing on adding-machine tape somehow caught her imagination, and that was enough to ignite her desire to write.

Learning to write is one of the great challenges of childhood. It takes time. It takes patience. Sometimes it takes adding-machine tape. And it always helps to have a game to play.

APPENDICES

A LIST OF IMPORTANT SPELLING WORDS

This list includes the 370 words that children use most often when writing. The list is divided into three parts: Easy Words, Tough Words, and Even Tougher Words. In deciding in which category to place a word, I considered both the difficulty in spelling and the frequency with which children employ the word when they write. That is why *come*, a word that is hard for many children to master, is an Easy Word, while *last*, a simpler word to spell, is a Tough one.

Easy Words

a	by	got	love	run
all	call	had	mad	sad
am	came	has	man	sat
an	can	hat	may	see
and	car	he	me	she
any	cat	hen	men	sit
are	come	her	met	six
as	dad	him	miss	so
ask	day	his	mom	stop
at	did	hit	must	sun
ate	do	home	no	ten
back	dog	hop	not	the
bad	end	hot	of	to
bag	fall	how	old	top
ball	far	I	on	up
bat	fast	if	one	us
be	fat	in	or	was
bed	fell	into	out	we
big	fish	is	pet	well
book	for	it	play	went
box	fun	let	ran	will
boy	get	like	rat	with
bus	go	look	red	yes
but	good	lot	ride	you

Tough Words

add	felt	hurt	now	such
ago	find	inside	off	take
air	fine	jump	on	that
baby	fire	just	our	them
began	five	keep	own	then
best	fly	kind	put	think
bike	food	last	real	this
black	forgot	late	said	told
both	from	little	same	too
bring	funny	live	saw	took
candy	game	made	say	toy
class	gave	make	seem	try
coat	girl	many	seen	two
cry	give	mice	self	under
doing	glad	mine	send	until
doll	gone	more	side	use
door	happy	most	sing	want
down	have	mouse	sister	was
drop	hello	much	small	way
each	help	name	some	what
eat	here	need	soon	who
every	hold	new	stay	without
face	hope	next	still	work
feel	house	nice	street	your

Even Tougher Words

about	along	around	behind	busy
across	already	away	believe	can't
afraid	also	became	below	care
after	always	because	blue	carry
afternoon	animal	become	broke	catch
again	another	been	brother	child
almost	answer	before	brown	children
alone	anything	began	build	city

clean	first	laugh	remember	those
close	found	light	right	turn
color	friend	making	sang	upon
could	goes	morning	school	very
dear	great	mother	show	wait
didn't	grew	move	since	walk
does	grow	near	small	wasn't
done	hard	never	snow	were
don't	high	night	something	we're
drive	how	nothing	store	when
easy	I'd	once	story	where
else	I'll	only	sure	which
enough	I'm	open	table	while
eyes	isn't	other	talk	why
family	I've	people	thank	woman
father	knew	rain	their	won't
few	know	ready	there	write
fight	large	really	these	you're

BOOKS FOR READING ALOUD

Here is a list of books you may enjoy reading with your child. A good read-aloud book should hold a child's attention, trigger his imagination, and please you, the adult, too. Some of the books on this list are short. You can read them in a single sitting. Others are chapter books that will take a week or more to complete. It may happen that you begin a book with enthusiasm but after several chapters you and your child become bored. There is only one thing to do under these circumstances. Stop reading the book and pick a new one.

I've arranged the books in five categories: fiction, fairy tales and mythology, nonfiction, poetry, and jokes and riddles. As much as possible, I've listed the selections in order of difficulty, beginning with the easiest. But you shouldn't take this aspect of the list too seriously. Younger children, when they are enthusiastic about a story, can follow even complicated plots.

Fiction

Caps for Sale by Esphyr Slobodkina
Cloudy with a Chance of Meatballs by Judith Barrett
Millions of Cats by Wanda Gag
Miss Nelson Is Missing by Harry Allard
The Story of Ferdinand by Munro Leaf
Madeline by Ludwig Bemelmans
Fortunately by Remy Charlip
My Mama Says There Aren't Any: Zombies, Ghosts, Vampires, Creatures, Demons, Monsters, Fiends, Goblins, or Things by Judith Viorst
It Could Always Be Worse by Margot Zemach
What Do You Say, Dear? by Sesyle Joslin
Catwings by Ursula K. LeGuin
The Crack-of-Dawn Walkers by Amy Hest
Bartholomew and the Oobleck by Dr. Seuss
Horton Hatches the Egg by Dr. Seuss
Many Moons by James Thurber

Crow Boy by Taro Yashima
The Stories Julian Tells by Ann Cameron
Old Mother West Wind by Thornton W. Burgess
Winnie-the-Pooh by A. A. Milne
The House at Pooh Corner by A. A. Milne
Stuart Little by E. B. White
Charlotte's Web by E. B. White
Jacob Two-Two and the Hooded Fang by Mordecai Richler
Mrs. Piggle-Wiggle by Betty MacDonald
My Father's Dragon by Ruth Stiles Gannett
Sarah, Plain and Tall by Patricia MacLachlan
Just So Stories by Rudyard Kipling
The Reluctant Dragon by Kenneth Grahame
The Cat Who Went to Heaven by Elizabeth Coatsworth
The Animal Family by Randall Jarrell
Abel's Island by William Steig
The Real Thief by William Steig
The Enormous Egg by Oliver Butterworth
The Devil's Storybook by Natalie Babbitt
Goody Hall by Natalie Babbitt
How to Eat Fried Worms by Thomas Rockwell
The Adventures of Treehorn by Florence Parry Heide
The Book of Dragons by E. Nesbit
Stories for Children by Isaac Bashevis Singer
The Mouse and the Motorcycle by Beverly Cleary
The Secret Garden by Frances Hodgson Burnett
The Borrowers by Mary Norton
Half Magic by Edward Eager
Homer Price by Robert McCloskey
Caddie Woodlawn by Carol Ryrie Brink
Song of the Trees by Mildred D. Taylor
Mr. Popper's Penguins by Richard and Florence Atwater
Soup by Robert Newton Peck
The Indian in the Cupboard by Lynne Reid Banks
The Half-a-Moon Inn by Paul Fleishman
The Chronicles of Narnia by C. S. Lewis
Harriet the Spy by Louise Fitzhugh

The Phantom Tollbooth by Norton Juster
Sounder by William Armstrong
The Thirteen Clocks by James Thurber

Fairy Tales and Mythology

The Classic Fairy Tales edited by Iona and Peter Opie
Jack Tales by Richard Chase
The People Could Fly: American Black Folktales by Virginia
   Hamilton
The Tales of Uncle Remus: The Adventures of Brer Rabbit by Julius
   Lester
The Dancing Kettle and Other Japanese Tales by Yoshiko Uchida
D'Aulaire's Book of Greek Myths by Ingri and Edgar Parin d'Aulaire
D'Aulaire's Norse Gods and Giants by Ingri and Edgar Parin
   d'Aulaire
The Juniper Tree and Other Tales from Grimm translated by Lore
   Segal and Randall Jarrell
The Maids of the North: Feminist Folk Tales from Around the World
   by Ethel Johnston Phelps
American Tall Tales by Mary Pope Osborne
American Tall Tales by Adrien Stoutenburg
Realms of Gold: Myths and Legends from Around the World by
   Ann Pilling

Nonfiction

The Magic School Bus series by Joanna Cole
Animals Do the Strangest Things by Leonora and Arthur Hornblow
Volcanoes by Franklyn M. Branley
My First Book About Space: A Question and Answer Book by Dinah
   L. Moché
Journey into a Black Hole Franklyn M. Branley
Anno's Counting House by Mitsumasa Anno
All in a Day by Mitsumasa Anno and others
Anno's Mysterious Multiplying Jar by Masaichiro and Mitsumasa
   Anno

How Much Is a Million? by David M. Schwartz
Mummies Made in Egypt by Aliki
Why Don't You Get a Horse, Sam Adams? by Jean Fritz
And Then What Happened, Paul Revere? by Jean Fritz
The Courage of Sarah Noble by Alice Dalgliesh
Cathedral: The Story of Its Construction by David Macaulay
Castle by David Macaulay
Wanted Dead or Alive: The Story of Harriet Tubman by Ann McGovern
Amos Fortune, Free Man by Elizabeth Yates
Make-Believe Empire: A How-To Book by Paul Berman
Ben and Me by Robert Lawson
Mr. Revere and I by Robert Lawson
Secret Missions: Four True Life Stories by Ellen Levine

Poetry

When We Were Very Young by A. A. Milne
Now We Are Six by A. A. Milne
The Random House Book of Poetry for Children selected by Jack Prelutsky
Oh, What Nonsense edited by William Cole
The Book of Pigericks by Arnold Lobel
The Hopeful Trout and Other Limericks by John Ciardi
Cats Are Cats edited by Nancy Larrick
Side by Side edited by Lee Bennett Hopkins
Sing a Song of Popcorn: Every Child's Book of Poems selected by Beatrice Schenk de Regniers, Eva Moore, Mary Michaels White, and Jan Carr
All the Small Poems by Valerie Worth
Spin a Soft Black Song by Nikki Giovanni
The Oxford Book of Children's Verse in America edited by Donald Hall

Joke and Riddle Books

Bennett Cerf's Book of Riddles by Bennett Cerf
Jokes for Children by Marguerite Kohl and Frederica Young

More Jokes for Children by Marguerite Kohl and Frederica Young Sterne

Faint Frogs Feeling Feverish and Other Terrifically Tantalizing Tongue Twisters by Lilian Obligado

Tongue Twisters by Charles Keller

Six Sick Sheep: 101 Tongue Twisters by Joanna Cole and Stephanie Calmenson

Eight Ate: A Feast of Homonym Riddles by Marvin Terban

World's Toughest Tongue Twisters by Joseph Rosenbloom

The Zaniest Riddle Book in the World by Joseph Rosenbloom

Tyrannosaurus Wrecks: A Book of Dinosaur Riddles by Noelle Sterne

A NOTE TO TEACHERS

There are many excellent ways for teachers to use the ideas and activities in *Games for Writing.* With a few simple adaptations, you can play any of the games in your classroom. In some cases, no adaptations at all are needed—for instance, if you are working with a single child.

Let us suppose that one of your students is having trouble coming up with a writing topic. Urge him or her to compose a MONSTER CAFE menu, or write A SILLY BOOK, or devise a BOARD GAME. You might teach the children to play FORBIDDEN LETTERS or IS IT TRUE? and let two or three of them play together on days when writing a story would require too much effort or concentration.

Many of the games are appropriate for small group work. A group of three or four children, with minimal instruction, can play EGG-CARTON TALES or THAT'S GOOD/THAT'S BAD without adult supervision. With six to eight children, you can create an ANGRY ALPHABET BOOK. Assign each of the children a few pages and then bind the completed text, which will delight the whole group.

Certain of the activities are suited for larger groups. You could bring your entire class together to create a SHE IS SO MEAN story. Go around the room asking each child to contribute a new wicked deed, which should be amusing. When the class has had enough, you could ask the children to write additional character studies on their own.

The organization of *Games for Writing* should make it easy to find appropriate activities for your class. Kindergarten and first-grade teachers should take a look at Part One, "Just for Starters." That section is intended to engage emergent writers in a variety of activities that promote both language and motor development. Read WRIBBLING, for example, and then try turning a corner of your classroom into a mini-restaurant. Your could show the children how to "wribble" menus, customers' orders, signs for daily chef's specials, and advertisements. After a week or so, you might transform the corner into a veterinary clinic with medical records and prescription pads on which the children will need to "wribble."

You can use THREE-COLOR ROAD RACE and OBSTACLE COURSE to help children refine their small-motor skills. Reproduce several copies of a single race. Give one copy each to four or five children and let them "race it out." You could teach OBSTACLE COURSE to your class. Show the children how to make a game sheet and explain the rules. Suggest that your students draw their own obstacle courses and use these courses to challenge their classmates.

You might help the children draw STORY MAPS and encourage them to label—with invented spelling—the various locations. Emergent writers, especially those who have not been read to extensively, need this kind of directed play. It will help them develop and internalize sophisticated notions of story grammar.

First-, second-, and third-grade teachers should look through Parts Two, Three, Four, and Five. In these sections, you will find games for children who already have some experience in writing. Teachers of primary-grade children need to help their students become relaxed and fluent at writing. And they need to help young authors learn to compose narratives that are interesting and well-defined. Parts Two through Five offer you a variety of playful ways to meet these twin objectives.

In every primary classroom, there are youngsters who find it hard to get started writing. These children will benefit from the "Stress Busters" found in Part Two. Even if you do not assign your children to write stories as a rule, you might consider using "Stress Busters" to reduce anxiety for worried young writers. If a child is overwhelmed at the prospect of telling a complete story, let him write something less daunting. Let him MAKE A LIST, compose an ACROSTIC POEM, or engage another writer in a LET'S ARGUE debate. Accomplished writers in your class will appreciate a stress-busting break in between longer projects.

Some of the games will prove useful for teaching spelling, grammar, and handwriting. You might include a few games from Part Three, "Bugaboos—Spelling, Handwriting, and Grammar," in your lesson plans. You may find that these games are appropriate for homework as well as class work. Several of the games in this chapter refer to the List of Important Spelling Words in the Appendix. To create this list, I've drawn on the Dolch list of common words, *3,000 Instant Words* by Elizabeth Sakiey and Edward Fry, (Providence, Rhode Island: Jamestown Publishers, 1984), and "The Basic Spelling Vocabulary List" developed by Steve Graham, Karen Harris, and Connie Loynachan (*Journal of Educational Research*, vol. 86, no. 6).

Your students will need lessons in character development and story grammar. Some teachers give such lessons in individual conferences; others prefer large group discussions. Whichever technique you use, you can incorporate an occasional game into your curriculum by using the activities in Part Four, "Writing with Style."

It is always a good idea for children to complete at least one major writing project during the school year. You will find suggestions for such projects in Part Five, "Made with Pride."

In addition to using the games in your classroom, you might consider introducing some of these activities to parents. The right kind of parent involvement can make a substantial difference in the education of young children, as several research studies have shown. So when a parent of one of your students asks, "Is there anything I can do to help my child?" you might want to respond with specific suggestions about useful games to play at home. You could present some of the games at parent meetings and conferences. Or invite the parents into your classroom to play with individual children. Not every parent will respond to the invitation, but even with two or three parents, you could organize some simple and interesting classroom activities.

The games in this book touch on many individual skill areas—story grammar, spelling, character development, organizational requirements, clarity of style, and so on. But the games do something else as well. They give children a wide array of enjoyable and productive writing experiences. To get children to do a little writing every day is a valuable thing. To get them not only to write but to love writing is more valuable still. *Games for Writing* can help you do just that.

Games Listed by Age Level

GAMES	K	1	2	3
Part One: Just for Starters				
Wribbling	★	★		
Three-Color Road Race	★	★		
Obstacle Course	★	★		
Just What I Said	★	★		
Catch My Silly	★	★		
Story Maps	★	★		
Read Aloud Plus	★	★	★	★
Say It with Pictures	★	★		
Write It for Me	★	★		
Popcorn Writing	★			
Pretzel Letters	★	★		
Part Two: Stress Busters				
Halting Stories		★	★	
Silence Is Golden		★	★	★
Monster Cafe		★	★	★
A Race of Words		★	★	
Word by Word		★	★	★
Make a List		★	★	
A Silly Book		★	★	★
Let's Argue			★	★
Do It		★	★	★
Schedules			★	★
Is It True?			★	★

GAMES	K	1	2	3
Part Five: Made with Pride				
Shape Books		★	★	★
Angry Alphabet Book		★	★	
Write a Letter		★	★	★
Board Games		★	★	★
Family Journal		★	★	★
Comic Books			★	★
Plays and Players			★	★
The Longest Story Ever Written		★	★	★